T0191181

Praise for *Love Has a Story*

In *Love Has a Story*, Quina masterfully combines biblical theology, storytelling, and personal poems to draw us closer to the God who is love. In discovering the magnificent love story of God throughout eternity and time we find that our own lives are also meant to be stories about God's love. This book is a gift.

CHRISTINE CAINE, founder of A21 & Propel Women

Quina's meditations are a dazzling gift. She effortlessly entwines her musings on Scripture with such unique poetic response that I found she left my heart and mind both unified and refreshed. I have spent years writing songs and stories trying to get across a singular point: God *is* relationship, and He longs to be in one with us. We are made by love for love. This is the driving force behind every word in this book, and it is, I believe, the single most life-changing discovery one can make. Quina's words are a gift to that end. Cherish this book. I know I have.

MIKE DONEHEY, author and frontman of Tenth Avenue North

Love Has a Story is a beautifully dynamic meditation on God's unstoppable love for us, as experienced specifically by Quina Aragon. The best stories make room for trials, triumphs, loss, and love. What you hold in your hands contains all of that in a bold blend of poignant poetry, powerful prose, and personal portraits—all presented through the lens of Scripture. Love has a story, and this wonderful work invites you into it.

RASOOL BERRY, Director of Content Development, VOICES from Our Daily Bread Ministries

In a fresh format, Quina invites you on a reflective devotional journey that incorporates Scripture, story, and poetry to help you become more of the type of human God desires us to be. These bite-sized devotionals can be done in a few minutes or carried throughout the day. Take up, read, reflect, and prayerfully rest in the goodness of God through this labor of love.

RAYMOND CHANG, President of the Asian American Christian Collaborative and Executive Director of the TENx10 Collaboration

Perhaps you've wondered why love feels impossible at times. The grudge you can't seem to let go of, or the words that tumble out, laced with anger instead of understanding. True love isn't a theoretical concept; it's a force in action. But a risky decision because love demands vulnerability. Quina lays herself bare—opening her life as an exhibition to the truth that Christ never overlooks an opportunity to satisfy a hungry soul. Her words offer us a most remarkable invitation: to experience the kindness of God.

RICH PÉREZ, filmmaker and storyteller

Quina Aragon's lyrical writing weaves poetry and Scripture to push our thoughts beyond our suffering. Her words, drawn from God's great love Story, linger in the soul and heal. Open this book, enter the Story, and receive this benediction.

K. A. ELLIS, Director, The Edmiston Center for the Study of the Bible and Ethnicity

Let's all admit it. The love of God can feel distant, unreal. We might even wonder, as I myself have wondered, *My life is such a disaster. Does God hate my guts?* Quina Aragon's *Love Has a Story* is for people like us. This book will move your heart, because it comes from Quina's heart. There is no pious spin here. *Love Has a Story* is for anyone who is open to the real love of God.

RAY ORTLUND, Renewal Ministries, Nashville

What distinguishes Quina's work is her exceptional talent for weaving the tapestry of her own personal battles with trauma, worry, and the dark nights of the soul to unveil a profound truth: God's love, boundless and embracing, not only cradles our deepest pains and insecurities but also breathes within them, gently shaping and transforming us amid life's tumultuous currents.

AMEEN HUDSON, writer, speaker, podcaster

LOVE

HAS A STORY

100 Meditations on the Enduring Love of God

Quina Aragon

MOODY PUBLISHERS

CHICAGO

Unless otherwise noted, Scripture quotations are from the ESV® Bible (The Holy Bible, English Standard Version®), © 2001 by Crossway, a publishing ministry of Good News Publishers. Used by permission. All rights reserved. The ESV text may not be quoted in any publication made available to the public by a Creative Commons license. The ESV may not be translated in whole or in part into any other language.

Scripture quotations marked CSB have been taken from the Christian Standard Bible®, Copyright © 2017 by Holman Bible Publishers. Used by permission. Christian Standard Bible® and CSB® are federally registered trademarks of Holman Bible Publishers.

Scripture quotations marked (NIV) are taken from the Holy Bible, New International Version®, NIV®. Copyright © 1973, 1978, 1984, 2011 by Biblica, Inc.™ Used by permission of Zondervan. All rights reserved worldwide. www.zondervan.com The "NIV" and "New International Version" are trademarks registered in the United States Patent and Trademark Office by Biblica, Inc.™

Published in association with William K. Jensen Literary Agency

Edited by Pamela Joy Pugh
Interior design: Puckett Smartt
Cover design and image: Jon Aragón
Cover element of torn paper copyright © 2024 by ooddysmile/iStock (1031672574, 1031668972). All rights reserved.

Library of Congress Cataloging-in-Publication Data

Names: Aragon, Quina, author.
Title: Love has a story : 100 meditations on the enduring love of God / Quina Aragon.
Description: Chicago : Moody Publishers, [2024] | Includes bibliographical references. | Summary: "Before the foundations of the earth, the great storyteller was penning a story that included you. Love was thinking about you, imagining ways to showcase His love for you, and planning to rescue you. Enter the greatest love story ever told. You'll want to share this with friends and family"-- Provided by publisher.
Identifiers: LCCN 2023057610 (print) | LCCN 2023057611 (ebook) | ISBN 9780802425591 (hardcover) | ISBN 9780802476517 (ebook)
Subjects: LCSH: God (Christianity)--Love--Meditations. | God--Love--Biblical teaching. | Love--Religious aspects--Christianity--Meditations. | Love--Religious aspects--Christianity--Biblical teaching.
Classification: LCC BT140 .A67 2024 (print) | LCC BT140 (ebook) | DDC 231/.6--dc23/eng/20240329
LC record available at https://lccn.loc.gov/2023057610
LC ebook record available at https://lccn.loc.gov/2023057611

Originally delivered by fleets of horse-drawn wagons, the affordable paperbacks from D. L. Moody's publishing house resourced the church and served everyday people. Now, after more than 125 years of publishing and ministry, Moody Publishers' mission remains the same—even if our delivery systems have changed a bit. For more information on other books (and resources) created from a biblical perspective, go to www.moodypublishers.com or write to:

Moody Publishers
820 N. LaSalle Boulevard
Chicago, IL 60610

1 3 5 7 9 10 8 6 4 2

Printed in China

To Jael.

Remember: Mommy loves you, Papi loves you, but guess what?
Jesus loves you even more.

To every curious and aching heart, like mine.

May this offering grant you greater certainty of the love story
God has written and *is writing* through you.

CONTENTS

PART THREE

The Corruption of Our Love and Your Story's Great Conflict

PART FOUR

The Mysterious Migrations of Love

PART FIVE

Love's Rescue and Rule, Your Progressing Plot

PART TEN

The Community of Love and Your Story's Non-Ending End

I am grateful to have been loved, and to be loved now,
and to be able to love, because that liberates. Love liberates.

DR. MAYA ANGELOU

A Note to the Reader:
Love Has a Story,
and You're a Part of It

It's been said that the revelation of God is progressive. As you read the story of Scripture, the very character and plan of God unfolds like a blooming rose. By the end of the story, the glory of God shines so bright, you almost regret comparing it to a rose—even the reddest of roses.

The Bible's story, of course, is the greatest story ever told. It involves a King, a bride, a betrayal, a ransom, and a great wedding feast. Told another way, it involves a Father, a lost child, and an unthinkable adoption. Or you can say it's a story about the lengths someone went to make His enemies His friends. The Bible's story can be summarized in various ways using various major themes, but there can be no doubt that it is, in every sense, a love story.

The greatest love story ever told.

Or like the lyrics my Puerto Rican grandmother, affectionately called "Mamita," used to sing:

"Es la historia de un amor, como no habra otra igual."[1]

"It's a love story, like no other that will ever exist."

Story is core to our humanity. Communications theorists go so far as to use the term *homo narrans*—storytelling humans—to describe the primacy

---

1   "Historia de un amor," Carlos Eleta Almaran; editorial Mexicana De Musica Int. S. a. (emmi), Southern Music Publishing Co. Ltd.

of storytelling to human identity.[2] An old African proverb seems to have summarized this well: "Share the facts, and I'll learn. Tell the truth, and I'll believe. Tell a story, and I'll be forever changed."[3]

God is a storyteller. *The* storyteller. And, as it turns out, "God is love" (1 John 4:8, 16). Holy love is central to God's very identity (Ex. 34:6–7). And how does He choose to show us this? Through the grand story of Scripture. Through this story we learn that the Creator of the universe is, at His core, covenantal. This means His aim has *always* been relationship. "You shall be my people, and I will be your God" is His repeated chorus. So the Bible is a story about God, yes. But that's not all. The Bible is a story about God *and* us; it's a story about God *with* us. Scripture is a story we're not merely meant to read and memorize but to experience, embody, and even continue.

Have you ever seen your life as a story in itself with a greater story (God's) embedded within it? Have you been so swept up into God's story that your own no longer feels flat, random, or a mere tragedy? Do you see how your own life story—every paragraph and chapter, every mundane task and unspeakable misfortune—might echo, in its own unique way, *the* great love story?

Could you have the courage to believe love has a story, and you're a part of it?

I want to invite you to explore God's love as it has existed and moved throughout and before time, and how it intends to transform your own life story. This is, obviously, something no mere one hundred meditations could ever suitably unpack. At the end of the apostle John's account of Jesus, he states: "Now there are also many other things that Jesus did. Were every one of them to be written, I suppose that the world itself could not contain the books that would be written" (John 21:25). God's love is a story we will explore for all eternity. But my prayer is that this book—whether you read it in one sitting or one hundred—will offer you a bit of footing, a

---

2 Carl Rhodes and Andrew D. Brown, "Narrative, Organizations and Research," *International Journal of Management Reviews* 7, no. 3 (2005): 167–88, doi:10.1111/j.1468-2370.2005.00112.x

3 Exact attribution and articulation of this proverb is unknown. Some say it is actually an indigenous American proverb.

bit of companionship, and more than a bit of hope as you traverse Scripture's story—and yours.

My prayer is "that you, being rooted and grounded in love, may have strength to comprehend with all the saints what is the breadth and length and height and depth, and to know the love of Christ that surpasses knowledge, that you may be filled with all the fullness of God" (Eph. 3:17–19). Did you hear that? It takes divine strength to comprehend divine love. Being totally soaked in the experience of God's love isn't something PhDs, or perfect church attendance, or even this book can accomplish in you. So whether you currently feel irrepressibly inflamed by God's love or something more like a frozen flint of jaded cynicism—or somewhere in between—do pray for the Holy Spirit's help as you turn the pages of this book. Even a short (or silent) prayer like, "God, help," is felt and heard by the Spirit, who "helps us in our weakness" and "intercedes for us with groanings too deep for words" (Rom. 8:26)

One more thing. Many of the poems you'll find interspersed throughout this book are those I've performed as a spoken word artist. If you think it would help you engage with these parts of the book, I invite you to visit LoveHasAStory.com to hear my voice.

Now let's begin, shall we?

But First, a Confession

But first, I must now confess to you something you'll see in some of my own personal poems interspersed through this book. I sometimes—and sometimes *more than* sometimes—have a very hard time viewing my own story as redemptive.

In my darker moments, I find myself standing in the shadowy hallway of traumas I've suffered, many of which compounded just as soon as I first trusted in Christ at age sixteen. I hear whispers, and sometimes shouts, that I'll never escape this hallway. I see doors open in this hallway and the shadowy figures of my reenacted traumas, the abandonments, the emotional abuse, the sexual abuse, the spiritual abuse, the overwhelming regrets—all poking out. I struggle to see any door with a bright green Exit sign.

I experience chronic nightmares, intrusive thoughts, emotional flashbacks, and struggles with hypervigilance and a sense of worthlessness. I slip into dissociated states and fight/flight/freeze defense mechanisms more than I would ever want to admit to you. In those moments/days/months, I hardly hear God's love singing over me. Instead, I hear: "You'll never escape," and "You're a worthless failure." Sometimes, even: "God isn't here. He's not even real."

I suffer from a mental health condition called complex post-traumatic stress disorder (CPTSD), which can develop when a person experiences chronic (long-term) trauma and stress. For most of my teenage and adult years, I assumed my intense difficulty with emotion regulation, sense of self, and relationships was just a matter of being a really bad Christian. I didn't understand how prolonged traumatic stress had affected my brain's chemistry and nervous system. I knew that Jesus died for my participation in evil acts, words, and thoughts. But I didn't understand—at least not experientially—how Christ's incarnation spoke to the goodness of my body, how His crucifixion spoke to His solidarity with abuse victims, and how His resurrection spoke to the promise of the future healing and transformation of my damaged mind, soul, body—*and* story. I didn't understand how His resurrection power, even now, includes His still-scarred hands touching my own scars, bringing life out of my worst wounds . . . like Him.

My faith in the gospel—the good news of Jesus Christ—was genuinely real but admittedly limited in scope. For the last five years, through compounded traumas that broke me in ways I'm still recovering from, God has graciously taken me on a journey of rediscovering my own story with the help of mental health professionals, loving church community, and much time spent wrestling, lamenting, and learning from "the God of all comfort" (2 Cor. 1:3).

In the middle of writing this book my back gave out, and I was told in the hospital I might die that night. I was discharged the next day with no diagnosis by a doctor who insinuated my back pain came from abusing drugs. Wild. As I spent every day going from specialist to specialist, disputing claims with my insurance, and trying to find ways to assuage the pain, I had to stop working altogether.

I've spent the last four years trying to finish writing this book while being (seemingly) interrupted by the intense grief of secondary infertility, four major surgeries for stage 4 endometriosis (resulting in the loss of six organs), a fifth surgery, debilitating and still-undiagnosed chronic back pain and fatigue, as well as the inconceivable loss of family and friends. Those losses are not all limited to death, by the way, but deportation, and with others, unresolved conflict. My stomach sinks even writing that.

This book was *supposed* to be a ten-month writing project. It has turned into a much bigger story for me.

One that has had me walk through the mystery and darkness of prolonged traumas.

One in which the silence of God became a psalm.

And ultimately, one that has written on my soul the steadfastness of God's love indescribably—more than I could ever write on paper, though I try.

Despite the many redemptive movements of God in my life in the last couple years of writing this book—including relocation, trauma therapy, family support, and even financial breakthrough—I've struggled to forgive, I've struggled with lust, I've struggled with intense bouts of anxiety and depression.

I've bucked against entrusting my story to our wonderful Wounded Healer.[4]

I've cursed in the darkness. I've cursed the darkness.

I've struggled to know in my bones the love of God.

How could I, someone who has verbalized more than once in the process of writing this book, "God hates me. He wants to kill me," and "The world is better off without me,"—how could *I* pen genuine words on the love of God? I've both cried and laughed as I've asked myself this question.[5]

So, I hope you'll indulge my tendency to struggle *and* to believe through the poeticizing of parts of my own journey. I hope you'll hold the pieces of my story gently, as I hope you'll find Christ's scarred hands doing the same for you—bringing forth life from death, love from shame's depths.

---

4   I borrow this phrase, "the Wounded Healer," from Henri Nouwen's book *The Wounded Healer: Ministry in Contemporary Society* (New York: Image, 1979), which years ago set me on a path to seek professional help in discovering and finding a measure of healing for my emotional wounds and life story with the renewed hope that my wounds—when better understood, articulated, and tended to by the Holy Spirit and in safe relationships—might actually serve as healing agents for this world (Christ, of course, being the ultimate Wounded Healer).

5   If you or someone you know needs help, please call or text the 988 Suicide and Crisis Lifeline.

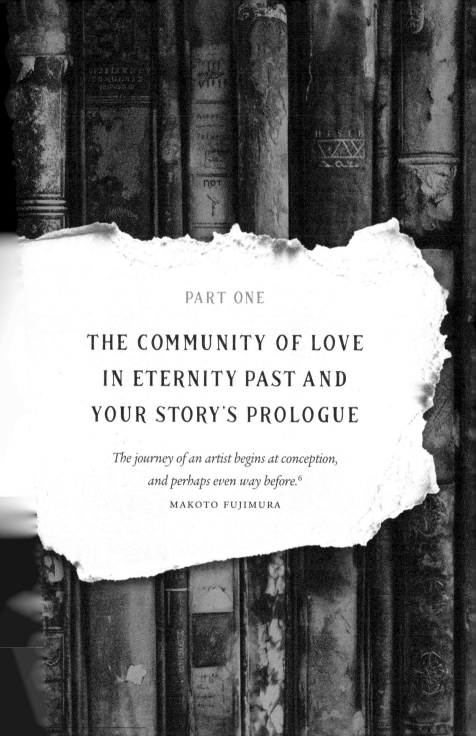

PART ONE

THE COMMUNITY OF LOVE
IN ETERNITY PAST AND
YOUR STORY'S PROLOGUE

The journey of an artist begins at conception,
and perhaps even way before.[6]

MAKOTO FUJIMURA

Makoto Fujimura, *Art and Faith: A Theology of Making* (New Haven, CT: Yale University Press; First Edition, 2021), 1.

Before Creation, a Community

"Father, I desire that they also, whom you have given me,
may be with me where I am, to see my glory that you have given me
because you loved me before the foundation of the world."

JOHN 17:24

Before the morning dew glistened on blades of grass, before mountains stretched their necks to peer into the clouds, before a single creature breathed or blinked, there was God—One who has eternally existed as the Father, the Son, and the Holy Spirit. And, according to Jesus' prayer in John 17, what pumped through the metaphorical veins of that three-in-one glory was . . . love.

Love has no birthday. God is eternal—He has no beginning and no end (Ps. 90:2). And, the apostle John tells us, "God is love" (1 John 4:8).

So before time was,
there was Love.[7]
And before creation,
 a community.

It may seem overly ambitious to begin a hundred-day meditation on the love of God with such an ineffable, mysterious doctrine as what is typically called "the Trinity." God's triune nature—one God forever existing in three Persons—is something we can't possibly comprehend in full, nor

---

7   Quina Aragon, *Love Gave: A Story of God's Greatest Gift* (Eugene, OR: Harvest House Publishers, 2021), 2.

should we. Our efforts to explain God's three-in-one-ness through analogies and metaphors fall short. We do well to listen to our Indigenous brothers and sisters along with early Jewish Christians in holding "the mystery of God in tension" rather than assuming we can pick apart and precisely analyze the divine.[8]

Yet it is here, in the diverse yet unified, eternal relationship between Father, Son, and Spirit—the "triune Community-of-Love"[9]—that we discover the very foundation of love.

REFLECTION

How does it land on you that at the center of the universe *is* relationship—that your desires for connection and relationship are rooted in the very nature of God?

8   Randy S. Woodley, "Beyond *Homoiousios* and *Homoousios*," in *Majority World Theology: Christian Doctrine in Global Context*, ed. Gene L. Green et al. (Westmont, IL: InterVarsity Press, 2020), 27.

9   Ruth Padilla DeBorst, "Church, Power, and Transformation in Latin America," in *Majority World Theology*, 498.

The Foundation of Love

Now when all the people were baptized, and when Jesus also
had been baptized and was praying, the heavens were opened,
and the Holy Spirit descended on him in bodily form, like a dove;
and a voice came from heaven,
"You are my beloved Son; with you I am well pleased."

LUKE 3:21-22

God has always lived in a diverse yet unified community of love:

> The Father loving the Son
> and the Son right back,
> the Spirit rejoicing in it all
> A perfect love union,
> forever intact.[10]

The Son tells the Father, "You loved me before the foundation of the world" (John 17:24). The Father tells the Son, "You are my beloved Son; with you I am well pleased"—with the Spirit descending as an expression of the Father's love, anointing Jesus for ministry (Luke 3:22).

The unbridled, unmerited delight of parent for child is but a whisper of a greater love. The substance from which all shadows of human love are cast is the utter delight of God the Father for God the Son, "who is in the

---

10 Quina Aragon, *Love Made: A Story of God's Overflowing, Creative Heart* (Eugene, OR: Harvest House Publishers, 2019), 22.

bosom of the Father" (John 1:18 NKJV[11])—right there affectionately reclined on His Father's chest, even before any creative act is achieved. Beloved before building a single thing. Imagine that.

Before any living creature breathed, there was God: loved and loving. The Trinity is the foundation of love. After all, could God truly *be* love if, within Himself, He did not exist in a diverse yet unified relationship? How could He *be* love without someone *to* love? God must *be* a community (Father, Son, and Spirit—perfectly unified) in order to *be* love.

So we begin here, in the God-occupied prologue of history—eternity past—where love was already alive and well in the community of the divine. Yet, as you know, every story must move beyond its beginning. And love, by nature, spreads.

But we've only just begun.

REFLECTION

What's one of the purest, most delightful moments of genuine love you've experienced or witnessed? How might that relationship or moment of love reflect something of the eternal love within the Trinity?

---

11 Scripture taken from the New King James Version © 1982 by Thomas Nelson, Inc. Used by permission. All rights reserved.

Eternal Love Origins

So Jesus said to them, "Truly, truly, I say to you, the Son can
do nothing of his own accord, but only what he sees the Father doing.
For whatever the Father does, that the Son does likewise.
For the Father loves the Son and shows him all that he himself is doing."

JOHN 5:19-20

Before God was Creator, He was Father.[12] And He was Son. And He was the Holy Spirit. And there He was: love.

Augustine, that fourth-century North African bishop, spoke of the Trinity as the Lover (the Father), the Beloved (the Son), and Love (the Holy Spirit).[13] In other words, the Father has always burst with delight in His Son, who perfectly reflects the Father's perfections (Heb. 1:3). Or as Jesus, the Son of God, said, "the Father loves the Son" (John 5:20). This love that flows from the Father to the Son by the Holy Spirit is no new phenomenon. It's been God's MO since before time.

All good and well and dusty-library-book worthy, but what does this have to do with your story and mine? Everything.

"For the Father loves the Son and shows him all that he himself is doing" (John 5:20). Just as back in Jesus' day a son learned his trade from his father who showed him the ropes of that trade, so the Son of God

---

12 Michael Reeves, *Delighting in the Trinity: An Introduction to the Christian Faith* (Downers Grove, IL: IVP Academic, 2012), 21.

13 St. Augustine, "On the Trinity," in *Basic Writings of St. Augustine*, vol. 2, ed. Whitney J. Oates (Grand Rapids, MI: Baker Books, 1992), 687.

has always perceived the Father's purpose and plan—including His plan to bring you and me into His family . . . even at the cost of the Son's life (Ps. 2:7–8; Isa. 53:10–11; Acts 2:23).

Everyone has an origin story. Perhaps you tend to think of your origin story as beginning at your birth, or your upbringing in your family of origin, or even with your ancestors' stories. But what difference does it make to know that your story actually has its origins in the eternal love of God the Father for God the Son?

A love that has no beginning. A love that planned all along to bring you into its story.

REFLECTION

How do you tend to tell your origin story, that is, where the story of your life/journey began?

Ocean Origins

I don't remember
the first time my toes
touched the elusive line
where sea meets sand.
Mom says it was Cocoa Beach
there with the whole family—
titas, titos, cousins, and my lola
    (you better never call her lola
    or *abuela*, by the way
    it's "Mamita" because
    she's forever young.
    don't say I didn't warn you.)
and that sounds about right to me.

Mom says I was wobbling my way to her
when I fell and found out
sand sticks to skin like a tan
and they had to turn away
so I wouldn't see them giggle
at my discovery.
They weren't cruel, they just knew me—
barely two, already very shy
"very strict" as my mom puts it
I didn't like any signs
of failure in me
to be seen.
But despite the sandy eyes
or the time I picked up a whole jellyfish
because I thought it was "litter"

(selah)

those moments
on the shore

were shalom.
they're scattered in the film reel of my
core memories,
little glass bottles floating
on my mind's coast
filled with the feeling
of sweet humidity
and a salty breeze.

My body remembers everything.
there's no number to the times
I've let it lead me
to the closest beach
just to breathe, *really breathe*
again.

They say time is a colonial construct
a history of empires burdening us
with a tyrannical need
for more and more productivity
and maybe just maybe
we should learn from the tides'
push and pull
cyclical like life
dangerous and beautiful
unrushed, unrelenting
like love.
Lately I've wondered how much
our enchantment with
certain types of terrain
and landscapes
trace back to where our ancestors'
feet once trod.

is it the Taino blood flowing in me
when I dance on underwater
sand dunes?
is it the Arawak Maroons
in my bones that make me
fearless of fierce waves?
is it the unknown
West African tribe
from whom my great-Jamaican-child
  of enslaved-
grandma ("Ma Black Eye")
descended, making this melanin
embrace UV rays
like a hug?
does my love
for kayaking, paddle boarding
awaken my arms in a way
only my river-dwelling Bikolanos
DNA could explain?
on my back, I let my flat feet kick
then I sink
as the water sings

welcome home, Pacific queen
of the Philippines, babalik karin
you are known, Atlantic-grown
hija querida de Arecibo,
Puerto Rico—come,
let me comb your Caribbean curls,
my Kingston girl

and whisper mysteries of victories
between bubbly breaths
let Ivory Coast dreams
sync your heartbeat
to African rhythms . . .

It's not a real beach visit
if I don't swim, float, or
(if it's really too cold)
at least dip my toes
in the ocean
we like to pretend
is split into four or five
when it really, like me,

is one. [14]

---

14 This is an original poem, but my inspiration here regarding our perceived need for more and more
    productivity comes from *Sacred Belonging: A 40-Day Devotional on the Liberating Heart of Scripture* by
    Kat Armas (Grand Rapids, MI: Brazos Press, 2003), 126–29.

The Son's Reward: *You*

"All that the Father gives me will come to me,
and whoever comes to me I will never cast out.
For I have come down from heaven, not to do my own will
but the will of him who sent me.
And this is the will of him who sent me, that I should lose nothing
of all that he has given me, but raise it up on the last day.
For this is the will of my Father, that everyone who looks on the Son
and believes in him should have eternal life,
and I will raise him up on the last day."

JOHN 6:37-40

In eternity past, as God existed in a perfect community of love—Father, Son, and Spirit—He mapped out the means by which you and I would be rescued from our sin and brought into loving, eternal fellowship with God (John 6:38–40).

Like an expert novelist, God outlined history before a page of it was ever written.

The Father decreed that He'd send His beloved Son on a rescue mission (John 8:42).

The Son agreed to this blood-soaked mission in loving submission to the Father (Phil. 2:5–11).

The Spirit would be sent out by the Father and the Son to apply the benefits of the Son's obedience to none other than . . . us (Rom. 8:9–17).

In Christ, your story is a love story that didn't start when you first believed. It didn't start at the cross of Christ. It didn't even start when God made the universe. Your story began within the counsel of the three-in-one God who determined to show off the immensity of His love by giving us His "only Son" (John 3:16), and by giving us *to* His Son as His inheritance (Eph. 1:18).

So before God promised people a Savior (Gen. 3:15), He promised His Son a people to save and treasure forever. And that people, dear friend, includes you.

Some call it the covenant of redemption. I think I'd call it the pre-temporal-inter-Trinitarian-sacrificial-love-pact. But I suppose that's why I'm not a proper theologian of theology proper.

REFLECTION

Have you ever had a relationship in which you've felt genuinely treasured? How does it land on you when you hear that *you* are God's treasure? How does it feel to know that you (as in, you specifically) were considered a part of the Son's future reward, His very inheritance? Read Psalm 2:7–8, Luke 22:29, and Ephesians 1:18 to marvel a bit more.

DAY 5

Your Story's Prologue

Blessed be the God and Father of our Lord Jesus Christ,
who has blessed us in Christ with every spiritual blessing in the heavenly places,
even as he chose us in him before the foundation of the world,
that we should be holy and blameless before him.
In love he predestined us for adoption to himself as sons through Jesus Christ,
according to the purpose of his will, to the praise of his glorious grace,
with which he has blessed us in the Beloved.

EPHESIANS 1:3–6

Can you imagine receiving a letter with an introduction as dense as this? It may help us to first notice the Trinity in this passage above: "the God and Father of our Lord Jesus Christ"; Christ, "the Beloved"; and the Holy Spirit[15] who transfers to us "every spiritual blessing."

Some have compared the simultaneous diversity and unity within the Godhead to a symphony—different notes and chords move to the same melody. As we've noted, though, analogies like these fall short when trying to explain the mystery of the Trinity.[16] But take this as a simple illustration of the harmony within the divine—each Person playing a particular role in creation and redemption with a unified purpose. And this symphony of glorious love, as we've already learned, began way before God was ever Creator.

---

15 Perhaps by implication, but more explicitly in verses 13–14.

16 This analogy, for example, doesn't account for the fact that God is not divided into three Persons as a symphony is composed of various instruments. Each Person of the Trinity is fully God, not a part of God.

In this passage, God the Father planned our salvation. The Son, in joyful submission to the Father, purchased, or achieved, our salvation. The Spirit, sent by the Father and the Son, preserves, i.e., seals, our salvation. Or put another way, the love that has eternally flowed from the Father to the Son by the Spirit, also flowed to us—even "before the foundation of the world."

If you're standing right now, you might want to sit down for a second. Did you know that if you're a Christ follower today, it's because God—according to His own free will—chose to set His eternal, unfailing love upon you before He created a single thing?

This is the prologue to your story, the beginning before the beginning. And it's glorious.

Before you danced in your mother's womb, before Adam and Eve, your greatest-grandparents, ever walked the earth, before stars lit up the night sky, there was God—handpicking *you* to inherit a bottomless ocean: His love.

REFLECTION

Sit with that phrase: "before the foundation of the world." That's the same phrase that describes God the Father's love for God the Son (Jesus) in John 17:24. But in this passage it's referring to *you*. How does God's electing love transform your thoughts about God's love for you? What types of questions might it provoke?

Chosen in Love

Blessed be the God and Father of our Lord Jesus Christ,
who has blessed us in Christ with every spiritual blessing in the heavenly places,
even as he chose us in him before the foundation of the world,
that we should be holy and blameless before him.
In love he predestined us for adoption to himself as sons through Jesus Christ,
according to the purpose of his will, to the praise of his glorious grace,
with which he has blessed us in the Beloved.

EPHESIANS 1:3–6

Can you imagine spending only one day in this glorious passage? What strikes me about it is its lack of apology or argumentation. That God chose us for salvation before creation and before we ever possessed any faith in Christ is stated so matter-of-factly here. That's not to say this teaching doesn't provoke worthy questions or concerns. But, for the moment, notice that Ephesians 1:3–14, which is one long sentence in the original Greek, showcases the proper response to God's pre-creation love for us: explosive praise!

When Paul says, "Blessed be the God and Father of our Lord Jesus Christ," he's saying, "Praise God the Father! Proclaim His supreme worth!" Why? Because He has blessed us in His Beloved Son to receive "every spiritual blessing," which includes our election, adoption, redemption, forgiveness of sins, wisdom and understanding of God's ultimate purpose in history, sealing by the Holy Spirit, and an inheritance. All of these blessings are blessings because they give us eternal access to God as our loving Father, Christ as our loving Savior, and the Spirit as the loving presence of God in us.

If your life is a story, then its prologue includes the moment God penned your name on the Lamb's book of life—"before the foundation of the world" (Rev. 13:8) . . . with indelible ink.

You might wonder (as I do), *Why, God? Why me?! Surely it's not because I would fill some sort of lack in You. And I wouldn't have surrendered to You if You hadn't first sought me. I don't possess something more special within myself than any other person. So why hand-select me to be forever engulfed in your love?*

He gives us no answer except "according to the purpose of his will, to the praise of his glorious grace" (Eph. 1:4–6). "Our God is in the heavens; He does whatever He pleases" (Ps. 115:3 NASB[17]). And what pleases Him is showcasing the wonders of His love. He loved you because He loved you because He loved you.

You know where to find the origin of God's lavish love toward you in Christ? Nowhere within you. And, if you let it sink in, that's the best news you'll hear today.

REFLECTION

If God does whatever He pleases, and what pleased Him was to set His love upon you since before time, how might He feel to see you trusting that you are loved by Him today? Can you imagine anything more heartbreaking for God than His children not believing He loves them?

---

17 Scripture quotation taken from the (NASB®) New American Standard Bible®, Copyright © 1960, 1971, 1977, 1995, 2020 by The Lockman Foundation. Used by permission. All rights reserved. lockman.org.

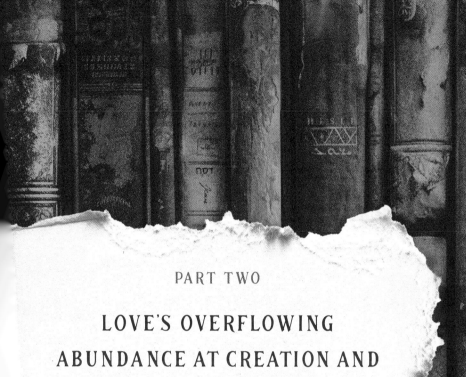

PART TWO

LOVE'S OVERFLOWING ABUNDANCE AT CREATION AND YOUR STORY'S INTRODUCTION

*Perhaps the mission of an artist
is to interpret beauty to people, the beauty
within themselves.*[18]

LANGSTON HUGHES

Langston Hughes, *Selected Letters of Langston Hughes* (New York: Knopf, 2015), Kindle, 54.

When Love Overflowed

The LORD is gracious and merciful,
slow to anger and abounding in steadfast love.
The LORD is good to all, and his mercy is over all that he has made.

PSALM 145:8–9

What was God up to before He spoke those famous first words, "Let there be light" (Gen. 1:3)? As we've seen, God wasn't bored. In that unified community of love—Father, Son, and Spirit—God suffered no lack or loneliness. Before He put on the hat embroidered with "Creator," God already wore a hat that said "Loving Dad."

But here's the thing about love: by nature, it moves outward. It spreads. Have you met a loving mom who *didn't* want to share pictures of her baby, along with stories of how he sneezed, smiled, and performed other bodily functions? Of course not! Likewise, a smitten bride tells anyone who will listen, "This is my beloved and this is my friend" (Song 5:16). Love seeks to let others in on its delight. It says, "Taste and see" (Ps. 34:8)!

Think for a moment about the beauty and complexity the earth possesses. The way nature, including the innumerable galaxies of our universe,[19] is all interconnected—from the way subatomic particles like protons, neutrons, and electrons work within atoms, to the way ecosystems of plants, animals, weather, and landscape collaborate with the energy of the sun to

---

19 NASA/Goddard Space Flight Center, "Earliest Strands of the Cosmic Web," ScienceDaily, June 29, 2023, www.sciencedaily.com/releases/2023/06/230629173611.htm.

maintain life here. The psalmist implies that the heart of God—"abounding in steadfast love"—is the impetus behind "all that he has made" (Ps. 145:8–9).

Creation is an act of the ultimate Artist making—not out of a sense of scarcity, not merely for utility—but out of the superabundance of His delight. Like an artist who feels that electrical impulse within her to create a poem, a painting, or a play, God made the universe out of His own enjoyment. Here's what I'm saying: the joy God had within Himself was so great and so exquisite, He let it spill over into what we call creation.[20]

REFLECTION

Your lived experience as part of the created world is participation in the overflow of God's love. What does it feel like to participate in God's love?

---

20 See my children's book, *Love Made: A Story of God's Overflowing, Creative Heart* (Eugene, OR: Harvest House Publishers, 2019), for a poetic presentation of this same truth.

Creation Sings God's Love

Give thanks to the LORD, for he is good,
for his steadfast love endures forever....
to him who by understanding made the heavens,
for his steadfast love endures forever;
to him who spread out the earth above the waters,
for his steadfast love endures forever.

PSALM 136:1, 5-6

The biblical writers don't let us get away with treating the creation account like a news report ("Loving God Creates Universe" . . . "Oh, that's nice. Can you pass the sugar, babe?"). God's creative act should cause us to quite literally stop and smell the roses because they whisper—no, sing—a special secret: "His steadfast love endures forever" (Ps. 136:6).

The Bible begins with a poetic, songlike creation story in Genesis 1:1–2:3 broken down into seven days.[21] On Days 1 to 3, God creates three habitats: day and night, the sky above and seas below, and dry land. On Days 4 to 6 God creates inhabitants for the three habitats: the sun and moon rule the day and night, the birds and fish fill the sky above and the sea below, and land animals fill the dry land. The story's climax is on Day 6 when, after creating the animals, God creates humans—male and female—in His image to lovingly rule over the earth's inhabitants and their habitats. Then on Day 7, God rested. Like an ancient Near Eastern

---

21 Or Genesis 1:1–2:4, depending on which scholar you ask.

king, God sat enthroned over His peaceful, idyllic empire.

The theological agenda behind this creation story wasn't to communicate precisely *how* God made everything nor to give a geological account of dinosaurs. Rather, it told the newly freed-from-Egyptian-slavery Israelites *who* God is and *how He relates* to His creation—particularly, that He is the one true God who created everything without any outside help and without any rivals to His sovereign rule.[22] The psalmists reflected on this creation story so we would "give thanks to the LORD, for he is good, for his steadfast love endures forever" (Ps. 136:1; also see Pss. 19, 104, 145).

In other words, creation sings of God's love, and it beckons us to join the chorus. Can you count every sunset you've ever seen? Every time you've heard a bird "sing among the branches" (Ps. 104:12)? Every cloud stretched out on its sky-bed? Sometimes we forget these many witnesses to God's love dancing around us day by day like falling autumn leaves.

What if we danced too?

REFLECTION

How might you delight in God's love today by enjoying His creation? Perhaps you could take a walk and thank Him for the colors you see and the sounds you hear, or sing praise to Him as you gaze at the stars, or spend extra time smelling a delicious meal before you say grace, or simply take a very deep breath and appreciate the air . . . God's air.

---

22 Sandra L. Richter, *The Epic of Eden: A Christian Entry into the Old Testament* (Downers Grove, IL: IVP Academic, 2008), 92–118.

Chasing My Wildest Dream
(Portrait of Jael, Almost Age 3)

You lie down
and softly ask for "leche"
it's your way
of coping with
our twelve-hour separation.
I say,
"OK, I'll get you leche,"
but leave you to
soon drift to sea—
　　a dream world awaits . . .
I wonder what you
think about in your crib,
suspended between
your dark room
and the colors of your imagination.
Wonder how
you rise with so much
eagerness in your eyes, all to do
the same thing.
The morning routine
brings you a joy
I think only God,
who tells the sun to rise
around the same time
every morning, fully gets.

Later,
I spin around, sweating brow
fixing dinner and the house
while you splash in the sink
"washing" your hands, laughing
at your reflection.
Busy me, dizzying "priorities"

'til tarried by a tug
on my shirt,
enough times for me
to peer down and see
saucer-wide, bright eyes
my wild child
my lightweight, great gravity
ready to play with Mommy.
I often think I ought to soar
out there (or at least
finish these chores)
but you ground me,
literally.
You won't stop tugging down
On my hand 'til I'm
on the floor
pretending to be a horse,
then a dog,
then an elephant.

Lately,
I get paid for my imagination and
chasing dreams is great
except
when I forget
my wildest dream is
already a reality
standing in front of me,
messy hair
gapped teeth
laughing
ready to be chased.

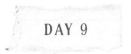

God's Loving Care for Creation

The heavens declare the glory of God,
and the sky above proclaims his handiwork.

PSALM 19:1

Remember how God called all His creation "good" (Gen. 1:21, 25)? The psalmist picked up on this goodness and saw fit to "sing to the LORD" (Ps. 104:33).[23] Poetry is meant to be read slowly. So take your time with this technicolor display of God's loving care for creation:

You make springs gush forth in the valleys;
    they flow between the hills;
they give drink to every beast of the field;
    the wild donkeys quench their thirst. . . .
From your lofty abode you water the mountains;
    the earth is satisfied with the fruit of your work.
You cause the grass to grow for the livestock
    and plants for man to cultivate . . .
The trees of the LORD are watered abundantly,
    the cedars of Lebanon that he planted.
In them the birds build their nests . . .

---

23 There is still goodness in the created order, despite the curse that came upon it when Adam and Eve sinned (Gen. 3:17–18).

O Lord, how manifold are your works!

In wisdom have you made them all;

the earth is full of your creatures. . . .

These all look to you,

to give them their food in due season.

When you give it to them, they gather it up;

when you open your hand, they are filled with good things.

(Ps. 104:10–11, 13–14, 16–17, 24, 27–28)

Clearly, creation wasn't made solely for mankind's needs. The psalmist depicts undomesticated animals (not seemingly useful to humans) as recipients of God's tender care and delight. Even the Leviathan (whale) was formed to "play" in the sea—or, if translated differently, God created the Leviathan to be His not-so-little plaything (v. 26)![24] Can you imagine having a pet whale? Apparently God can!

Humanity isn't God's only creation with intrinsic value. And utility isn't the Creator's only purpose for creation. The horse's gallop, the dolphin's dance, the butterfly's flutter—they all testify to something greater than practicality. They testify to God's great "pleasure in all he has made" (Ps. 104:31 NLT[25]).

REFLECTION

When you have a hard time finding words to pray, take a walk or look out a window and begin naming things you see—that tree, that squirrel, that bird. Begin thanking God for His loving care of those things. Take some time this week to try this. God's love is here, too.

---

24 ESV alternate rendering of Psalm 104:26: "There go the ships, and Leviathan, which you formed to play with."

25 Scripture quotation marked (NLT) is taken from the *Holy Bible*, New Living Translation, copyright ©1996, 2004, 2015 by Tyndale House Foundation. Used by permission of Tyndale House Publishers, Carol Stream, Illinois 60188. All rights reserved.

Our Loving Care for Creation

The creation itself will be liberated from its bondage to decay
and brought into the freedom and glory of the children of God.

ROMANS 8:21 NIV

I s our care for animals and the environment somehow connected to God's love? It's not a stretch to answer, "Yes!" From the beginning, God crowned humans as lowercase kings and queens "over the fish of the sea and over the birds of the heavens and over the livestock and over all the earth and over every creeping thing that creeps on the earth" (Gen. 1:26). Adam (meaning *earth* or *soil*) and his wife, Eve, were meant to care for the ground from which they came (see Gen. 1:26; 2:7–8, 15). Our care for creation is meant to be a reflection of God's.

God preserved the animal kingdom during the flood (Gen. 6:19–20) and included them in the Noahic covenant (Gen. 9:9–10). He gave the Sabbath laws that allowed animals rest (Deut. 5:14–15), forbade the boiling of a young goat in its mother's milk (a violation of the natural order; Ex. 23:19), forbade Israelites to kill a mother bird with her young (which would lead to that species' extinction; Deut. 22:6–7), and forbade the muzzling of an ox that is treading out grain (entitling food to the ox as it worked; Deut. 25:4). A righteous person is one who regards the life of his beast (Prov. 12:10). And have you considered God's concern for the cattle that would be destroyed if He visited Nineveh with judgment (Jonah 4:11)?

Then notice God's loving care for the environment in His command for Adam to "work" (serve) and "keep" (protect) the Garden of Eden (Gen. 2:15). Or the Sabbath laws that allowed the land to rest (Ex. 23:10–12). Or the law that required the practice of sustainability in warfare by not destroying trees that produce food (thus forbidding environmental terrorism; Deut. 20:19). The portrait of a righteous man is one who practiced sustainable farming (i.e., fallowing; Job 31:38–40).

You and I weren't meant to exploit creation—the land, the ocean, the animals—as though the earth were ours to devour rather than steward. We're meant to use all our senses to *delight* in His creation, all our creative capacities to *care* for His creation, and all our hearts to *praise* our loving, generous God who made it all. After all, the redemptive work of Jesus Christ won't only guarantee *our* resurrection but *creation's* as well (Rom. 8:18–25; Rev. 21:1; 22:1–2). Could it be that your story is actually connected to the story of nature—even the lions, tigers, and bears (oh my!)?

REFLECTION

Concerns like climate change and conservation have become politically charged terms in some circles. But how might the passages referenced above shape (or reshape) your attitude toward creation care?[26] How might you enjoy God by enjoying His creation today? How might you love God by caring for His creation today?

---

26 I highly recommend Sandra L. Richter's excellent book *Stewards of Eden: What Scripture Says About the Environment and Why It Matters* (Downers Grove, IL: IVP Academic, 2020) for further contemplation.

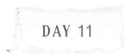

Crowned by Love

> O LORD, our Lord,
> how majestic is your name in all the earth! . . .
> When I look at your heavens, the work of your fingers,
> the moon and the stars, which you have set in place,
> what is man that you are mindful of him,
> and the son of man that you care for him?
> Yet you have made him a little lower than the heavenly beings
> and crowned him with glory and honor.
>
> PSALM 8:1, 3–5

It's now the second part of Day 6 in creation's songlike story. Suddenly, God breaks His pattern of creating habitats (Days 1 to 3) and their inhabitants (Days 4 to 6). His voice booms, "Let Us make mankind in Our image, according to Our likeness" (Gen. 1:26 NASB). If the cosmos had a jaw, this is when it dropped.

A king in the ancient Near East was considered an earthly representative of a particular deity with authority to act on its behalf. He would place statues of himself throughout his territory to indicate his sovereign rule and protection over that land. Everywhere the king's image was, so was his reign. But who is like the King of the cosmos? Our God made every single human—man, woman, rich, poor, young, old, fully able-bodied or not—in His image as His royal representatives (partners, if you will) on earth.

God's blessing to "be fruitful and multiply and fill the earth and subdue it" (Gen. 1:28) would empower humans to cultivate and govern the earth until the Garden of Eden—the place (temple) where God dwelt—was broadened and broadened and BROADENED until the whole earth was "filled with the knowledge of the glory of the LORD as the waters cover the sea" (Hab. 2:14).[27]

How can God, whose fingers crafted the stars, assign so much dignity to a species made of dust (Gen. 2:7)? How can He who made massive elephants and whales choose to "put all things under [*our*] feet" (Ps. 8:6)? Apparently, God's majestic character is revealed in the way He uses weak, seemingly insignificant things—yes, us—to display His powerful dominion.

God continues to work in this way throughout the story of Scripture. Why? "So that no human being might boast in the presence of God" (1 Cor. 1:29).

REFLECTION

In what ways does God's love humble us? In what ways does His love exalt us? Why is it important for us to acknowledge both of these realities?

---

27 I poetically summarize the *imago Dei* (image of God) in my spoken word short film "Listen and Live," https://youtu.be/U5wYDSio4eA.

Wanted: The Great Introduction of Your Story

And God saw everything that he had made, and behold, it was very good.

GENESIS 1:31

Like an artist beholding his masterpiece, God beheld all He made and declared: "very good." This "very good" wasn't a declaration of functionality (as a manufacturer might declare about the capability of a machine) but a declaration of delight (as you would proclaim, with sauce still on your face, about an exceptional meal, like my mother-in-law's *sancocho*).

So here's the great introduction of your story: you are wanted. God didn't *need* to make you, but He *wanted* to make you. He didn't create you as a mere slave to fill some sort of lack within Himself, but because He wanted you to share in the overabundant love He has for His Son (John 17:23, 26; 2 Cor. 4:6). Author Michael Reeves explains: "Why might God decide to have a creation? One of the earliest attempts at an answer can be seen in ancient Babylon's creation myth, *Enuma Elish*. There the god Marduk puts it bluntly: he will create humankind so that the gods can have slaves. . . . most gods since have tended to like his approach."[28]

Nonbiblical creation stories involving a one-person deity (or warring deities) can't possibly claim to have created us out of a generous overflow

---

28 Michael Reeves, *Delighting in the Trinity: An Introduction to the Christian Faith* (Downers Grove, IL: IVP Academic, 2012), 39–40.

of love. That's why understanding God as a perfectly unified, eternal community of love (the Trinity) is crucial to understanding our own origin story. We were made out of the overabundance of the "triune Community-of-Love"[29]—not His lack and certainly not under compulsion. Out of God's delight and desire, you and I were masterfully knit together in our mothers' wombs (Ps. 139:13).

If you're breathing right now, you can confidently declare: "I am wanted."

REFLECTION

Whether you were born to loving parents, abusive parents, or parents you've never known, you weren't made by accident but intentionally by Love Himself. Do you feel like this truth affirms, or perhaps rubs up against, what you've experienced to be true? If you were to write the "Introduction" of your life story, how would this truth shape what you say?

---

29 Ruth Padilla DeBorst, "Church, Power, and Transformation in Latin America," in *Majority World Theology: Christian Doctrine in Global Context* (Westmont, IL: InterVarsity Press, 2020), 498.

Crafted by Loving Hands

O Lord, you are our Father; we are the clay, and you are our potter;
we are all the work of your hand.

ISAIAH 64:8

Perhaps you read the creation account of Genesis 1 and find it too abstract, too ancient, or too grand—not personal enough to move you. God made everything. "Cool." He made humans in His image. "Okay." What does that have to do with my self-destructive habits? My childhood trauma? My tendency to look in the mirror and see someone I detest?

If the creation account in Genesis 1:1–2:3 tells us about our transcendent God—a God who is above and beyond His creation—then the complementary creation account of Genesis 2:4–25 reveals that God is also, shockingly, immanent. He is a God intimately involved with and near His creation.

Like a craftsman, God "formed the man of dust from the ground" (Gen. 2:7). Like a gardener, He "planted a garden in Eden" where He put the man (Gen. 2:8). Like a builder, He made the man's rib into a woman (Gen. 2:22).

Have you ever seen a skilled potter, clay underneath his fingernails, totally focused on the lump of soil between his hands? Have you ever seen a gardener, like my husband's Colombian *abuela*, singing to her flowers as she waters them in the morning? Have you seen a sweaty, disheveled mother burst into tears of joy as she holds her newborn, placenta-plastered baby on her chest?

These kinds of labors look a lot like love, don't they? This is the kind of meticulous, intentional, loving care with which God made His images—us.

What circumstances, harmful words, or family stories cause you to doubt that you were crafted by loving hands? What parts of your body, your emotions, or your story are hard for you to see as crafted by God's loving hands?

To My Inner Child

Younger me,
I hear you speak
when I come out to play
when these old bones
jump, explore
stare at the magnificent green
of leaves on a bright day
I feel your tiny, dimpled hands
holding mine
through my raw longings—
your vulnerability, your curiosity
make every moment
a poem,
no verse restraints.
I can almost hear you sing
sans insecurity
when I dig through the soil
or beach mud
the dirt beneath my nails become
a manicure the color free
I smell like "outside"
and you just beam.
You're my favorite me, I think.
and in a moment
I can't decide: smile or cry?
that I'm not busy scolding you
for all you "should" be.

DAY 14

A Big Deal to God

For we are His workmanship [His own master work, a work of art],
created in Christ Jesus [reborn from above—spiritually transformed,
renewed, ready to be used] for good works.

EPHESIANS 2:10 AMP[30]

Some of my favorite fictional stories are the ones where the protagonist is a nobody in society—an orphan, a slave, a poor kid, a misfit. Then, to everyone's great surprise, a messenger comes to inform him that he's actually a very important somebody—a prince, a prophesied deliverer, an heir. The protagonist then struggles to believe such great news. It disrupts his self-worth, his perceived origin story, his very identity. It *must* be too good to be true. The protagonist must grow into his newly discovered value. It doesn't happen overnight.

When you're born on the "wrong" side of town, with the "wrong" skin color, to the "wrong" parents, with the "wrong" interests, you're made to feel that the very essence of who you are is, well, wrong. But what if the origin story hiding beneath your perceived origin story whispers something of incredible worth and intricate design? An identity of immeasurable value you get to grow into—a masterpiece (Eph. 2:10; Col. 3:10).

What does it mean to be successful or valuable in your society? And what does it take to be a "powerful" or "impactful" man or woman of God? Heather Thompson Day quotes Pastor Ronnie Martin in her book *It's Not*

30 Amplified Bible by The Lockman Foundation, La Babra, CA 90631. All rights reserved.

Your Turn as saying: "If we're being honest, the desire to do 'big things for God' is a convenient way to mask our desire to do big things, God or no God."[31] Perhaps beneath this desire is some measure of "I just want to feel like my life counts, like I'm seen and valued." But what if doing "big things for God" (or at least how many of us have imagined it—broad recognition, sales, and enterprise) is much *less* than what you're called to? What if fame, "impact," or "reach" doesn't make you more valuable in the eyes of your loving Creator? What if you're *already* a big deal to God?

What if, because of the image of God already on us, our prayers of, "Lord, let my life count," were transformed into, "Lord, help me see how much my life *already* counts"?

> Every moment—mundane, maddening, magical—holy, wholly His.[32]
> Every chapter in your story already written, yet
> mysteriously unfolding
> with your God-given agency
> to coauthor with Him.

> Maybe that's the story the world needs to read.

REFLECTION

> How might your sense of value and beloved-ness change when you begin to pray, "Lord, help me see how much my life *already* counts"?

---

31 Heather Thompson Day, *It's Not Your Turn: What to Do While You're Waiting for Your Breakthrough* (Downers Grove, IL: IVP, 2021), 118.

32 "When your life seems insignificant": *Every Moment Holy: Volume 1* by Douglas McKelvey (Nashville, TN: Rabbit Room Press, 2017); *The Book of Common Courage: Prayers and Poems to Find Strength in Small Moments* by K. J. Ramsey (Nashville, TN: Zondervan, 2023); and *Liturgies from Below: Praying with People at the End of the World*, edited by Cláudio Carvalhaes (Nashville, TN: Abingdon Press, 2020).

The Title of Your Story

Beware lest you say in your heart,
"My power and the might of my hand have gotten me this wealth."
You shall remember the LORD your God,
for it is he who gives you power to get wealth,
that he may confirm his covenant that he swore to your fathers,
as it is this day.

DEUTERONOMY 8:17–18

The title of your story isn't meant to read "Self-Made Woman Makes a Name for Herself" or "How I Overcame, My Way."

Eve knew her ability to conceive and bear a child came "with the help of the Lord" (Gen. 4:1; cf. 4:25). Job knew it was foolish to kiss his own hand (take self-credit), as though God hadn't given him his strength, "hand," in the first place (Job 31:27). Moses warned the once-enslaved, wilderness-wandering Israelites to not assume that their own power or intelligence got them their wealth once they were settled in the Promised Land (Deut. 8:17–18). King David told God: "your gentleness made me great" (2 Sam. 22:36)—not David's wits, or his godliness, for that matter.

You were created for a glory greater than being the hero of your own story. If we are "more than conquerors," then it's only "through him who loved us" (Rom. 8:37). God, like a royal Father, crowned you "with glory and honor" (Ps. 8:5) according to His image because He loves you, and He loves to show what He can do with dust (Gen. 2:7).

God's love has certainly empowered His people to do some really heroic things (though I personally would prefer to not be put into a den of lions or a furnace of fire, but I digress). What are some moments in your story that you can now say: "I did/overcame/accomplished that only by the grace of God"?

If you were writing your memoir or autobiography, what would its title be? Get creative with it.

Love's Fingerprints

For you formed my inward parts;
you knitted me together in my mother's womb.
I praise you, for I am fearfully and wonderfully made.
Wonderful are your works;
my soul knows it very well.
My frame was not hidden from you,
when I was being made in secret,
intricately woven in the depths of the earth.
Your eyes saw my unformed substance;
in your book were written, every one of them,
the days that were formed for me,
when as yet there was none of them.

PSALM 139:13-16

In Toni Morrison's novel *The Bluest Eye*, a dark-skinned, African American girl named Pecola Breedlove is convinced that her mistreatment is because she is ugly. Her greatest ambition is to have blue eyes to make her beautiful and to cause her to see the world differently. What might the truth of the *imago Dei* (image of God), poetically pondered in Psalm 139, do to a wounded soul like hers? What about yours?

The great novelist James Baldwin once said, "Every human being is an unprecedented miracle."[33] This very truth is what caused King David to

---

33   James Baldwin, *No Name in the Street* (United States: Dial Press, 1972), 10, Kindle.

sing of God's careful craftsmanship of humanity. He compares God to a skillful weaver who intricately knitted him together in the womb.

The truth of the *imago Dei* on *all* human beings hasn't been easily accepted (even by Christians). History is filled with the dehumanization of the "other." But the *imago Dei* teaches us that God's fingerprints—fingerprints of love—are on our dark or light skin, our dreadlocked hair or bald heads. It teaches us that ethnicity, socioeconomic and immigration status, mental and physical capacity, and education level have absolutely no bearing on our immeasurable worth. It teaches us that the unborn—"intricately woven" in her mother's womb—is just as worthy of protection as those who have been born, and the value of the elderly is not diminished with their productivity.

The *imago Dei* teaches us that your life matters, and whatever ways society, community, or family devalues your full, God-given humanity, I must raise my voice to say, with Baldwin and King David: "Here is one of God's wonderful works, made with love! Treat her as such."

REFLECTION

How might you raise your voice to assert and defend the image of God on others this week? Perhaps you could address a racist comment a family member made, or financially support an organization that is serving a marginalized group, or participate in a food drive. The possibilities are endless.

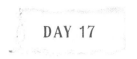

A Loving Author

In your book were written, every one of them,
the days that were formed for me,
when as yet there was none of them.

PSALM 139:16

The Bible begins with "God's people living in God's place with full access to his presence."[34] Holy love was the air Adam and Eve breathed. It was *shalom*—holistic, cosmic well-being, harmony, justice, love, and peace between all creation and its Creator. Perfect unity.[35] Glorious.

But in our next section we'll see how that cosmic *shalom* was shattered: God's love was questioned, doubted, and rejected by His image-bearers. What would come of God's love, and ours, as a result? How will we make it back to experiencing the fullness of God's love?

Before we explore that, sit with this quote from Dan Allender:

God is not merely the Creator of our life. He is also the Author of our life, and he writes each person's life to reveal his divine story. There never has been nor ever will be another life like mine—or like yours. . . . And God writes the story of my life to make something known about

---

34 Sandra L. Richter, *The Epic of Eden: A Christian Entry into the Old Testament* (Downers Grove, IL: IVP Academic, 2008), 98.

35 Many thanks to Pastor Ike Todd of New Creation Fellowship in Orlando, Florida, for helping me more clearly see God's plan (and the Bible's story) as one of "perfect unity."

himself, the One who wrote me. The same is true for you. Your life and mine not only reveal who we are, but they also help reveal who God is.[36]

What makes a story a story? It will include characters, a setting or location, a plot, a conflict, and a resolution (when the conflict is solved), or perhaps a catastrophe (conflict unresolved or worsened), or a cliffhanger. Of course, Scripture's metanarrative (the Bible's big story) isn't so much a story as it is history; its people not so much characters as they are real humans; its places not mere settings but actual geographic locations. The Bible is one big story, and what makes it so unbelievably beautiful is that it is, indeed, a true story—written by the same Author of your life's story.

What difference would it make if we embraced that the Author who wrote "the days that were formed for me, when as yet there was none of them" (Ps. 139:16)—that this Author *is* love (1 John 4:8, 16)?

REFLECTION

As you meditate on Psalm 139:13–16, jot down some of the major characters, setting(s), plot(s), and conflict(s) of your story so far.

36 Dr. Dan B. Allender, *To Be Told: God Invites You to Coauthor Your Future* (Colorado Springs, CO: WaterBrook, 2005), 3.

Mamita's House

Can you make it like it used to be?

peeling oranges and tangerines from
    Mamita's trees?

you can keep the grapefruit though, I'm
    good.

Tito Gary sings on the CD, Tita Horten
    is visiting

Lolo belts Sinatra, crunching on *chich-*
    arrones

meanwhile, we're being scolded

for playing in "the green room"

with the fancy pillows and

framed pics of their eleven kids

and countless grandchildren.

Tita Diane is helping in the kitchen

Tita Quela and Gabin are laughing
    about something

Tito Juan and Javi are visiting from
    Miami

Tito Andy and Robby make us all cry-
    laugh

you can hear my mom's voice from all
    the way in the back

(she's not even yelling)

Tita Liza and Gina are on the back porch

Tito Gary's watching the Bulls game, of
    course.

But I'm with my cousins

we're contriving a foolproof perfor-
    mance,

with choreography we'll convince our
    parents

to let us all sleep over.

The titas and titos sit at the "adult
    table"

(Mamita made the best pot roast again)

Unspoken rule: the loudest rules

they get to tell the story

with five other angles told
    simultaneously

good luck keeping up, we're

a dull roar continuously

Lolo's puns and Mamita's "Aha!" laugh
    interject

we're *halo-halo*, mix-mix

Tagalog and English

y un poco de español

I somehow follow the convos

but then get pulled

to play Sonic or cards

or learn a new dance move

(it's sad I still can't dance)

Mom lets Mo and me stay long

so we get to play mahjong

and eat *pakwan* seeds and all things salty

I take too long to build my mahjong wall
    (Mamita says)

excitedly shout, "*Pong!*"

but Tita Liza wins . . . again.

If I'm lucky enough to sleep over

there's fried egg and toast in the
    morning

and café con leche, *claro*

I might see Tito Gary reading his Bible

on the back porch

I'll probably see what Oita's doing today
or go play basketball with Gab at the park
you know,
another family beach day would be nice.
I kiss every cheek before I leave,
and Mamita's twice
she'll walk me out and
wave as I drive
away
I know we'll be back
next week, same time
I don't know "goodbye."

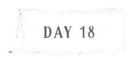
A Redemptive Arc

Bless the LORD, O my soul . . .
who redeems your life from the pit,
who crowns you with steadfast love and mercy.

PSALM 103:2, 4

The Bible is made up of many smaller stories that each play a role in developing the Bible's big story: God is redeeming a people for Himself through His Son in order to renew (resurrect) the entire universe—humanity and creation—in perfect unity and harmony under His loving kingship, for our good and for His glory. But what did it mean to "redeem" back in Bible times? Old Testament scholar Sandra Richter helps us:

> In Israel's tribal society redemption was the act of a patriarch who put his own resources on the line to ransom a family member who had been driven to the margins of society by poverty, who had been seized by an enemy against whom he had no defense, who found themselves enslaved by the consequences of a faithless life. Redemption was the means by which a lost family member was restored to a place of security within the kinship circle.[37]

Redemption meant good news for the poor, lost sons and daughters returned to the safety of their father's house, freedom from slavery, rescue

---

37 Sandra L. Richter, *The Epic of Eden: A Christian Entry into the Old Testament* (Downers Grove, IL: IVP Academic, 2008), 45.

from a strong enemy. Are you hearing echoes of the Bible's story of redemption? God has been writing a story that begins with the triune community of love and ends with all of creation joining in that community of love with perfect *shalom*. It's the ultimate love story, but it gets very ugly very quickly. Yet through the muck and mire of humanity's rebellion and its far-reaching effects, God writes history's plot with a redemptive arc.

You'll notice the Bible's overarching plot cycles over and over all the way to its end: creation, corruption, redemption, and new creation.[38] So just as the Bible begins with God's people living in His place with His presence, it will end there—except, the end will be even more glorious than the beginning. Could it be that your story, made up of many smaller stories, might follow the same pattern?

REFLECTION

What are some griefs you feel—from generational trauma, your own personal victimization, and/or your own cycles of sin? What difference does it make to believe that God is eternally invested in redeeming "your life from the pit," writing your story with a redemptive arc?

---

38 Special thanks to Pastors Rechab Gray, Ike Todd, and Demetrius Hicks of New Creation Fellowship in Orlando, Florida, for the phrasing of this paradigm.

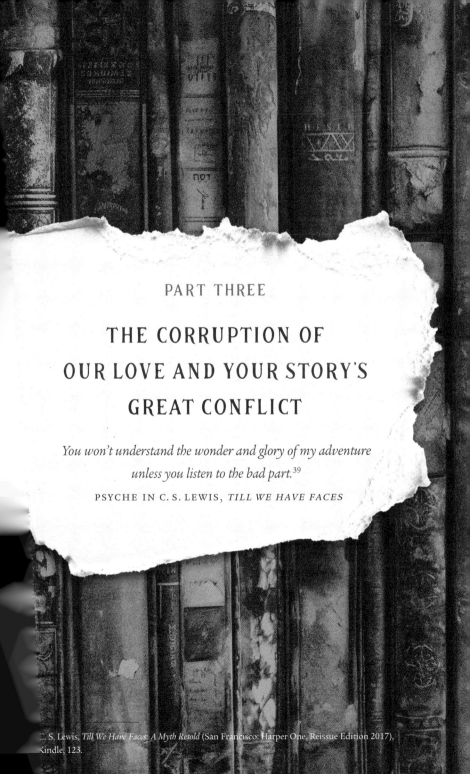

PART THREE

THE CORRUPTION OF
OUR LOVE AND YOUR STORY'S
GREAT CONFLICT

*You won't understand the wonder and glory of my adventure
unless you listen to the bad part.*[39]

PSYCHE IN C. S. LEWIS, *TILL WE HAVE FACES*

C. S. Lewis, *Till We Have Faces: A Myth Retold* (San Francisco: Harper One, Reissue Edition 2017),
Kindle, 123.

Our Story's Great Conflict

He said to the woman, "Did God actually say,
'You shall not eat of any tree in the garden'?"

GENESIS 3:1

Our story takes a sharp turn today. A great—*the* great—conflict is introduced as a new character slithers onto the screen. This "ancient serpent, who is called the devil and Satan, the deceiver of the whole world" (Rev. 12:9) was animated by anti-God, anti-good, anti-love power. And he was crafty.

Why did God allow evil to exist in the first place? The Bible doesn't tell us how good creatures—like Satan and a third of the heavenly hosts—could suddenly turn against God and choose evil (Luke 10:18; Rev. 12:3–9). Instead, it offers a story that explains our broken world. This problem of evil barreled through the hallways of history until it burst violently onto the cross of Christ—where the Son of God absorbed our evil and its consequences—to free us and His world from evil (Col. 2:13–15; 1 John 3:8).

But first, God commissioned that first love-made man (Adam) to be both gardener and guardian to the sanctuary park of Eden (Gen. 2:15). And his wife would partner with him in this work as "a helper fit for him" (Gen. 2:18). God told him, "You may surely eat of every tree of the garden, but of the tree of the knowledge of good and evil you shall not eat, for in the day that you eat of it you shall surely die" (Gen. 2:16–17).[40] Or more literally: "dying you shall die." If humanity's representative chose rebellion, the process of corruption and death would begin, in and around us all.

In other words, God said: "Go enjoy the exorbitant delicacies I've provided you on the menu. Eat, drink, and be merry in My love. But there's just one item on the menu you can't eat." That one item—the tree of the knowledge of good and evil—represented the choice mankind had. Would God or humans call the shots on what's good and what's not? In other words, who would get to be God in this world—God or us?

REFLECTION

Humanity's first conflict was a power struggle (us vs. God), when a whole banquet of love was offered. How do we sometimes choose power or control over love? How do you see that working out in society, organizations, your family?

---

40 "The man (Adam) receives this covenant on behalf of the rest of mankind: 'you' is singular in [Genesis] 2:16–17, which provides the basis for Paul's use of Adam as a representative head of the human race, parallel to Christ, in 1 Cor. 15:22; cf. Rom. 5:12-19." *ESV Study Bible* (Wheaton, IL: Crossway, 2008), 54.

A Question Mark on God's Love

They did not remember the abundance of your steadfast love, but rebelled . . .

PSALM 106:7

In ancient times, covenants—agreements between two parties with certain requirements and promises—were how the world was ordered. The suzerain/vassal treaty was one type of covenant in which a greater power (the suzerain) made a pact with a lesser power (the vassal), promising protection and provision in exchange for the vassal's tributes, military assistance, and a solemn promise to never, ever, *ever* serve a different suzerain. Loyalty to that covenant was something called *hesed*—often translated in the Bible as love, lovingkindness, kindness, mercy, or steadfast love (Ex. 34:6–7; Lam. 3:22–23; Mic. 6:8).

There is no perfect translation for the word *hesed*. That's because *hesed* communicates something far greater than what suzerain/vassal covenants could. Scripture's grand story reveals how God's defining characteristic is *hesed*—something much deeper than outward compliance to an agreement.

Still, keeping the covenant meant the vassal *loved* his suzerain; breaking the covenant meant the vassal *hated* his suzerain.[41] And so, those first humans had a choice: would they love their suzerain, or hate Him?[42]

Enter: the crafty serpent. If he could get them to doubt God's love for

---

41 Sandra L. Richter, *The Epic of Eden: A Christian Entry into the Old Testament* (Downers Grove, IL: IVP Academic, 2008), 69–91.

42 Even though the Hebrew word for covenant (*berit*) isn't in Genesis 2–3, God's interaction with Adam follows the pattern of covenant. In Hosea 6:7, God compares Israel's lack of covenant loyalty to Adam's lack of covenant loyalty.

them, then perhaps they'd feel justified in their rebellion (Ps. 106:7). His subtle misquotation of God's command essentially meant, "Is God *really* a good suzerain? It seems rather unloving of Him to deprive you like this."

> The serpent's sinister story of scarcity
> in God's good garden
> caused them to question
> Creator's intentions:
> can love really be love
> if it has boundaries?

The sentiment: "God doesn't love me, so I won't love Him" (the exact opposite of 1 John 4:19).

Cosmic treason ensued: "She took of its fruit and ate, and she also gave some to her husband who was with her, and he ate" (Gen. 3:6). And now, the sequence of authority established at creation was reversed: the "beast of the field" (Gen. 3:1; the serpent) undermined the humans' dominion, who then undermined God's. Everything upside down.

And then, "a terrible lie came into the world. . . . It would live on in every human heart, whispering to every one of God's children: 'God doesn't love me.'"[43]

Do you know that lie?

REFLECTION

What situations have you faced that made you think that perhaps that lie was true? How does that lie sometimes manifest in your life today? Consider the justifications you make when you choose to sin. Are you able to trace some of those justifications back to *God doesn't love me*?

---

43 Sally Lloyd Jones, *The Jesus Storybook Bible* (Grand Rapids, MI: Zonderkidz, 2007), 30.

The Warping of Our Love

In the last days there will come times of difficulty.
For people will be lovers of self, lovers of money, proud, arrogant,
abusive, disobedient to their parents, ungrateful, unholy, heartless,
unappeasable, slanderous, without self-control, brutal,
not loving good, treacherous, reckless, swollen with conceit,
lovers of pleasure rather than lovers of God.

2 TIMOTHY 3:1–5

Before Adam and Eve was the choice between life and death. To our detriment, they chose death. Though they didn't immediately suffer a physical death, no doubt a mercy, they were thrust from the realm of God's presence and pleasure, which, as you know, is life (Gen. 3:24; 1 John 5:12). And with this spiritual death came a tragic warping of our love.

In their fig-leaf-covered loins were now the DNA of our sexual, relational, generational brokenness, and overshadowing shame. Their healthy self-esteem, or self-love, which once flowed from an unhindered relationship with God, was now distorted. Their love for God was also warped. Look at them hiding from the One who made them to know His love (Gen. 3:8). Don't we hide, too—fig leaves of religiosity, or success, or so-called enlightenment insufficiently covering our shame?

Look at Adam blaming his wife, and not-so-subtly blaming God, who gave her to him; his wife blaming the serpent (Gen. 3:12–13). Hear the cries of painful parenting, oppressive marriages, disharmony with nature, frustrating work, and, ultimately, death (Gen. 3:16–19).

Watch humanity deep dive into depravity. Adam's son Cain murders his own brother Abel—as the blood of the victimized continues to cry out from the ground to this day (Gen. 4:1–10). Cain's descendant Lamech boasts of murder to his two wives—as misogynistic, domineering leaders continue to be exalted today (Gen. 4:23–24).

What has happened to our love, once pure and true? Have we not become shattered mirrors, reflecting mere fragments of God's love? In a world of warped love, might love still be the answer?

REFLECTION

What are some ways you've most painfully witnessed love being warped? In what ways is your own love for God, yourself, and others distorted?

Why is it important for us to examine our own wounds (some caused by others, some caused by ourselves), wrought by warped love?

Lust is a cheater

My Longing
met
my Lust
on the corner
of 5th and Pain.
They argued, then kissed—
it was complicated.
I should've known
Lust was a cheater, though.
After their embrace,
told Longing,
  "One sec, my Juliet."
just to
  text
  my irked Thirst
  some slick line
  about an escape, an "escapade"
  like, "you're missing out, mami"
shut the cellphone's screen
wiped the browser's history
so Longing couldn't see anything
then smirked
like,
  "I only got eyes for you, babe.
  Para siempre."
But wait,
Lust never called Longing "babe."

Plus, Thirst had heard
that word before: "escapade"
  last time Lust played her, in fact:
    offered her drinks
    just to leave her mouth
    feeling as if
    filled with sand.

(that's actually when Thirst
and Shame became
friends.)

Something in Lust's smile, though,
and that tone, oh,
that soft offer to "just relax"
just a quick little fix—a trance,
then . . . a relapse.

Next day,
Thirst caught Longing
at a café
weeping with my Grief
over coffee
too bitter to drink
sitting next to Shame
(Thirst didn't even know
Grief by name.)
All the same,
when Thirst walked in,
the barista's anxious eyes
revealed what they
already suspected—
they'd all been gulled.

Left that spot together
Thirst, Longing, Shame, Grief
arms linked
on their way
to a safer place,
to 7th and Mercy

limping
to Love.

— *Lust is a cheater, after all.*

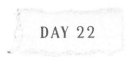
Love's Plot Twist

Has his steadfast love forever ceased? Are his promises at an end for all time?

PSALM 77:8

We just considered the cosmic consequences of humanity's rebellion against God. But we missed something. Even in this darkness, God's love shines as a light at the end of the tunnel of history—and all throughout that tunnel, too. Did you see it?

Before God declares the consequences of humanity's corruption, He curses the serpent: "I will put enmity between you and the woman, and between your offspring and her offspring; he shall bruise your head, and you shall bruise his heel" (Gen. 3:15). There is a promise in this serpent-directed curse for all who will hope in it: one day, an offspring of the woman will deal a deadly blow to evil, though it will cost Him . . . a lot.

The rest of the Old Testament will trace the lineage of that serpent-crushing seed of Eve, until a poor, virgin woman is told by an angel: "You will conceive in your womb and bear a son . . . and of his kingdom there will be no end" (Luke 1:31, 33). In His judgment, God remembered mercy (Hab. 3:2). This Son would do what Adam failed to do: slay the snake (Heb. 2:14–15). God would make war—"not *with* Adam and Eve but *for* them."[44]

This promise seems to motivate Adam to call his wife Eve, "the mother of all living," (Gen. 3:20) and Eve to acknowledge the Lord as she names her

---

44 Courtney Doctor and Melissa Kruger, *Remember Your Joy: Stories of Salvation* (Austin, TX: The Gospel Coalition, 2021), 6.

sons (Gen. 4:1, 25). Isn't that what hope does—invades our perspective, our decisions, even our name?

And so, in a *shalom*-broken world, the promise of *shalom* for the *shalom*-breakers beamed through the thick fog of their shame. The battle lines were drawn when Adam chose loyalty to the serpent. But behold, an almost-too-good-to-be-true plot twist: in this battle, the hero would die for the villains. Love would conquer. God promised it.

REFLECTION

We tend to cast ourselves as the hero or the victim in the stories we tell. But Scripture casts us as both victimizers *and* victimized in this broken world (Ps. 25:18–19; Matt. 8:16; Titus 3:3–5). Why do you think it's important for us to hear the promise of God's love when we've absolutely blown it and also when we've been wounded by others who have absolutely blown it?

DAY 23

A Love That Covers

Love covers a multitude of sins.

1 PETER 4:8

Did you think Genesis 3:15—that first gospel proclamation—was the only shining light of God's love in this tragic chapter of our history? Look again.

At the end of the creation account, we're told, "the man and his wife were both naked and were not ashamed" (Gen. 2:25). Sadly, in their desire to be "like God" (Gen. 3:5)—really, to *be* God—Adam and Eve forfeited their chance at donning royal and priestly garbs, which would have been theirs had they walked in righteousness (cf. Ex. 28:2; Rev. 5:9–10; 19:8).[45] Once likely radiating light like their Father (Ps. 104:2; Matt. 17:2), Adam and Eve now looked down at their bare nakedness and felt, for the very first time, nakedness in a new way: shame (Gen. 3:7; cf. 2:25). The emperor's emissaries had no clothes.

Their fig-leaf loin coverings weren't sufficient, not just because they were (probably) itchy in all the wrong areas. Sin—people's "bad hearts and broken ways"[46]—had crept into their souls, and with it, pervasive, haunting shame. Why else would they hide from God behind the trees (Gen. 3:8)? Ed Welch defines shame as "that all-too-human experience of

---

45 Nancy Guthrie, *Even Better than Eden: Nine Ways the Bible's Story Changes Everything about Your Story* (Wheaton, IL: Crossway, 2018), 62–63.

46 Matthew 1:21; *First Nations Version: An Indigenous Translation of the New Testament* (Downers Grove, IL: InterVarsity Press, 2021).

worthlessness, failure and not belonging."[47]

If guilt tells us we've done something bad, shame tells us we *are* bad, dirty, and unlovable—irredeemably so. Shame names us.

But God, in His love, covers Adam and Eve with the skins of an animal—an innocent animal that had to shed its blood for their covering (Gen. 3:21). The rest of the Old Testament would develop this concept of sacrificial atonement—the life blood of innocent animals would cover our guilt—until "the Lamb of God, who takes away the sin of the world" (John 1:29) would be abusively stripped (John 19:23), and would shed His precious blood to clothe us "with the garments of salvation" and cover us "with the robe of righteousness" (Isa. 61:10).

And so, the righteous judgment of God on our rebellion is sandwiched between two glaring demonstrations of His love (Gen. 3:15, 21). What does this tell us? The first and final word of our story is love—more than we could've ever bargained.

Reflection

Does it upset you that an innocent animal—a creature God created, takes pleasure in, and cares for—had to die in order to cover the guilty Adam and Eve? It upsets me. How does it make you feel, then, to know that the sinless Lamb of God (Jesus) died for *your* sins and *your* guilt (1 Peter 1:19; 3:18)? What do you think our tendency to dress fancily for special events, and our nightmares of being naked in public, tell us about our collective story as humans? Read 1 Corinthians 15:52–53, 2 Corinthians 5:1–4, and Revelation 19:6–9 for further contemplation.

---

47 Edward T. Welch, "Scripture Is About Shame," April 14, 2016, https://www.ccef.org/scripture-about-shame/. See also Welch, *Shame Interrupted: How God Lifts the Pain of Worthlessness and Rejection* (Greensboro, NC: New Growth Press, 2012).

God Loves His Enemies

"You have heard that it was said,
'You shall love your neighbor and hate your enemy.'
But I say to you, Love your enemies and pray for those who persecute you,
so that you may be sons of your Father who is in heaven.
For he makes his sun rise on the evil and on the good,
and sends rain on the just and on the unjust."

MATTHEW 5:43-45

Genesis 3:15 promised a coming deliverer, and it also announced the two sides of an ongoing, epic war: team serpent and team serpent crusher—which is just a fun way to say "team God" since Satan has never been, and will never be, on equal footing with the sovereign Lord of the universe. The rest of the Bible is a story about the contention between these two teams.

Eve's firstborn son, Cain, murders his younger brother, Abel, in a fit of jealousy. After being unjustly bereaved, Eve gives birth to Seth, who marks a new lineage of "team serpent crusher" people (see Gen. 4:25-26). In its seventh generation, Cain's lineage descends into the murderous, misogynistic Lamech. But in the seventh generation of Seth, a man named Enoch "walked with God" in intimate friendship (Gen. 5:24), and he miraculously did not die. In Cain and Seth's lineages are the serpent's offspring and Eve's offspring—the two paths before us all.

Yet God does something shocking with Cain. He doesn't immediately kill him, just as He didn't kill Adam when he rebelled. Unlike Adam, though, Cain exhibits no remorse, no repentance, and no faith in the promise of Genesis 3:15. He shirks responsibility for his younger brother asking, "Am I my brother's keeper?" (Gen. 4:9), and he bucks against the consequence of his sin without even apologizing for it (Gen. 4:13–14). He's unabashedly on "team serpent," and he's sporting the captain armband.

While God sentences Cain to futile gardening and perpetual wandering —no small consequence—He also protects Cain by putting a visible mark on him so that no one should attack and kill him (Gen. 4:8–16). Cain continues steadfast in his corruption, but God maintains His promise of protection—marking this murderer with mercy. What is this mark but proof that God's love extends beyond those who've bowed the knee to Him?

REFLECTION

Why would God show love to His enemies? Why should you?

A Humanizing Love

"But love your enemies, and do good, and lend,
expecting nothing in return, and your reward will be great,
and you will be sons of the Most High,
for he is kind to the ungrateful and the evil."

LUKE 6:35

In Chinua Achebe's *Things Fall Apart*, a people group in southeastern Nigeria is torn apart by British colonial incursions in the 1890s. Reverend James Smith (one of the colonizers) is a man who "saw things as black and white. And black was evil. He saw the world as a battlefield in which the children of light were locked in mortal conflict with the sons of darkness."[48] As a result, his actions toward the non-Christian tribe was far from loving.

In *Jesus and the Disinherited*, Howard Thurman observed: "It has long been a matter of serious moment that for decades we have studied the various peoples of the world and those who live as our neighbors as objects of missionary endeavor and enterprise without being at all willing to treat them either as brothers or as human beings."[49] The historical maligning of the biblical story of conquering love to somehow justify white supremacy, economic exploitation, human trafficking (slavery), and political dominance stands in direct opposition to two of the most basic truths of Scripture: we are all made in God's image, and God loves His enemies.

---

48 Chinua Achebe, *Things Fall Apart* (New York, NY: First Anchor Books Edition, 1994), 184.
49 Howard Thurman, *Jesus and the Disinherited* (Boston, MA: Beacon Press, 2012), 12–13, Kindle.

Since the beginning, God has extended a patient love toward His enemies, "not wishing that any should perish, but that all should reach repentance" (2 Peter 3:9). For humans who've rejected the call to reflect God's love, God's daily love for them is surprisingly . . . humanizing. He lets His enemies feel the warmth of the morning sun massage their faces. He rains provision on the ones who deny Him.

Because of Adam's sin DNA passed on to us, you and I were born on "team serpent" (Ps. 51:5; Rom. 3:10–23). And every moment we were on that side of the battle line, God was actively, patiently loving us—providing every meal, every laugh, every breath.

REFLECTION

In light of Howard Thurman's words above, how can you show a dignifying love toward those who either (1) don't believe what you believe, and/or (2) have gone out of their way to bring harm to you? Maybe spend some extra time praying and seeking counsel for this one.

A Man (He Is)

I married a man
who may be dead
should another with a gun
perceive him a threat.
I married a man
who when he drives
sits next to anxious wife
glancing at rearview mirrors like
crystal balls—
blue and red lights
might mean his demise
she reminds him to sound polite
show both hands
try to smile, say "sir"
take the ticket as a gift
it stings less than the bullet
forget any diminished sense
of his
humanity
I just want him breathing.
I married a man
whose smooth, satin skin
shelters me in the night.
his voice, his grin
his everything excites me.
I married a man
who gave me a daughter
his attention and affection for her
soothe my own Daddy wounds
our daughter swoons
calls him "Papi" and
knows she's safe.
Why can't they?

Betrayed Love

But Noah found favor in the eyes of the LORD.

GENESIS 6:8

Something amazing happens in Seth's lineage (the lineage representing team God): "people began to call upon the name of the LORD" (Gen. 4:26). Trusting in that Genesis 3:15 promise, these people worshiped and sought God. Their lineage leads us to a man named Noah who "walked with God," like his ancestor Enoch (Gen. 6:9; cf. 5:24) and unlike the rest of humanity at that time (Gen. 6:1–7).

In Noah's day, "the earth was filled with violence" and great corruption (Gen. 6:11). Do you hear the cries for justice from those victimized by this violence? Humanity's corruption was causing a reversal of God's good created order—men not protecting women (Gen. 6:1–4), the rich not caring for the poor, the image of God being spat upon as their blood, like Abel's, cried out to God for justice "from the ground" (Gen. 4:10).

Imagine a renowned painter beginning his passion project—contemplating its dimensions, deciding the exact Pantone Matching System code of each color he'll use, then brushing the canvas with precise, intentional movements. He steps back to behold his masterpiece. A tear escapes his eye. It's his magnum opus. It is "very good" (Gen. 1:31).

Now imagine his beloved apprentice sneaks into his studio in the dead of night and defaces this painting with images and words I can't repeat here. The painter arrives at his studio in the morning to find his apprentice still there, now ripping through the canvas with a knife. What does that painter feel? Certainly anger, even wrath. Such an injustice calls for it.

But wouldn't he also feel a deep sadness, even a sense of regret, that this apprentice, whom he mentored and loved as a son, would violate his creation? Wouldn't he be "grieved . . . to his heart" (Gen. 6:6)? Isn't that what love feels in the face of such blatant betrayal?

REFLECTION

Maybe it's not so hard to remember when you were betrayed—by a friend, spouse, leader, or neighbor. What are some words that describe how it made/makes you feel?

Love's Judgment

The LORD is good,
a stronghold in the day of trouble;
he knows those who take refuge in him.
But with an overflowing flood
he will make a complete end of the adversaries,
and will pursue his enemies into darkness.

NAHUM 1:7-8

God's creative work is worth far more than yesterday's analogy of a painting. But what happens when God's priceless and loved image-bearers (His apprentices) are the defacers of His masterpiece?

The story of Noah, who "found favor in the eyes of the LORD" (Gen. 6:8) while the rest of the unrepentant world around him drowned,[50] illustrates something the prophet Nahum would later affirm: God's love isn't mere license for us to live in opposition to Him (2 Peter 2:5, 9–10). His love is a holy, jealous love—like the love of a good wife who won't wink at her husband's adultery. God's love requires allegiance, just as a loving marriage requires spousal fidelity. And although God will wait patiently for that allegiance, He won't wait forever. God's holy love necessitates "an

---

50 "Since the geographical perspective of ancient people was more limited than that of contemporary readers, it is possible that the flood, while universal from their viewpoint, did not cover the entire globe. . . . a huge regional flood may have been all that was necessary for God to destroy all human beings." *ESV Study Bible* (Wheaton, IL: Crossway, 2008), 62.

overflowing flood" of judgment for all who continue in their rebellion against Him, and thus, against love (Nah. 1:8).

To be clear, the flood's destruction was the tragic conclusion of what was already happening: God's good created order being reversed by His image-bearers. The flood wasn't about God simply losing His patience, but rather God finally giving to mankind what they were actively seeking through their violence and corruption (Gen. 6:11–13): life without Him, which, like the rush of destructive waters, is chaos and death (cf. Rom. 1:18–32). As C. S. Lewis once said: "There are only two kinds of people in the end: those who say to God, 'Thy will be done,' and those to whom God says, in the end, '*Thy* will be done.'"[51]

REFLECTION

> If you were the painter in that scenario, imagine a judge declaring, "I know he trashed your life's work, but it's all good, right?" as he, with a wink, let your apprentice walk free without any justice. How would you feel if God looked at all the genocide, racial injustice, and sexual abuse in this world and said, "It's all good"? Would you call that love? Why or why not?

51 C. S. Lewis, *The Great Divorce*, in *The Complete C. S. Lewis Signature Classics* (New York: HarperCollins Publishers, 2002), 506.

I Can't Breathe

the waters, O God, the waters
are alive
they swell into my
gaping mouth
all I breathe
is drowning me
my thoughts tsunami
I'm sunken, condemned
your eyes blink, a lighthouse
but I cannot breathe, Jesus,
I can't breathe.

Patient Love

The LORD passed before him and proclaimed,
"The LORD, the LORD, a God merciful and gracious,
slow to anger, and abounding in steadfast love and faithfulness,
keeping steadfast love for thousands, forgiving iniquity
and transgression and sin, but who will by no means clear the guilty,
visiting the iniquity of the fathers on the children
and the children's children, to the third and the fourth generation."

EXODUS 34:6-7

Earlier we learned that in Bible times, faithfulness to a covenant was called *hesed* (steadfast love). Noah showed *hesed* when he made the ark (Gen. 6:13–22; Heb. 11:7). But he then failed to show *hesed* when he passed out drunk (Gen. 9:20–21). Scripture's story is witness to the fact that the only One with perfect *hesed* is God Himself.

But notice that God keeps "steadfast love" (*hesed*) for a thousand generations, in contrast to the three or four generations on which He visits iniquity. God's natural inclination to show love doesn't rot with time; it has no expiration date. In contrast, God's inclination to rain down judgment is not something He utterly delights in. He takes "no pleasure in the death of the wicked" (Ezek. 33:11) and He "does not afflict from his heart" (Lam. 3:33; cf. Luke 19:41–44).

God's heart is abounding, overflowing, spilling over with *hesed*—"ready to forgive" (Neh. 9:17) all who turn to Him in faith. Even this "visiting the iniquity" (Ex. 34:7) doesn't mean God punishes kids for their parents' sins (see Deut. 24:16), but rather God brings His just judgment on the patterns of evil He sees repeated from one generation to the next—but only after waiting patiently for their repentance, even up to four generations of their sustained rebellion.[52] Truly, "love is patient" (1 Cor. 13:4).

God's patient love doesn't negate the urgency to turn from our sin and turn to Him "now," "today" (2 Cor. 6:2; Heb. 3:15). Instead, His patient love removes any hesitation or hindrance to our returning to Him:

> *I would return, but my sin is too great.*
> *This is the thousandth time I committed this sin.*
> *This particular sin was especially sinister.*
> *I'm suffering under the natural consequences of my own foolishness.*
> *I've made my bed. Guess I gotta lie in it.*

No, no, no. Heaven rejoices at your repentance (Luke 15). His patience is greater than generations, His anger slow to boil over, His arms ready to wrap you in lavish love. Is it too good to be true that God could be *this* patient? Only if you refuse to believe, like Noah's generation. But the better bet is to "Come and see" (John 1:46).

And *because* of His patience, the quicker the better.

REFLECTION

How does God's patience encourage us to come back to Him quickly after we've sinned or strayed, rather than continuing to stay away?

---

52 See Genesis 15:16; Luke 11:47–51; 2 Peter 3:9.

DAY 29

Unquenched Love

Many waters cannot quench love, neither can floods drown it.

SONG OF SOLOMON 8:7

The flood of Noah's day was not only about God's judgment (Luke 17:26–27). It was about God graciously preserving the human race, from which would come the One who would obliterate evil (Gen. 3:15; 1 Peter 3:20). In Scripture's story, judgment and salvation are almost always coupled. And in Noah's story is Scripture's story in miniature: creation (Gen. 6:9–10), corruption (vv. 11–13), redemption (Gen. 6:14–8:19), and new creation (Gen. 8:20–9:19). God washed away human corruption to renew the earth, rather than annihilating it. He reestablished His covenant with creation through a single man. Sound familiar at all? See Luke 22:20; Romans 8:19–23; Revelation 21:1–4.

Ancient Mesopotamian literature acknowledges a catastrophic flood that wiped out whole populations, but it attributes the flood to the gods' annoyance with the too-noisy humans.[53] While those accounts exalt a human hero, the Bible exalts God's renewing mercy and enduring kindness, which "is meant to lead you to repentance" (Rom. 2:4).

There was only one thing left unrenewed by the deluge: humanity's heart, "evil from his youth" (Gen. 8:21). The terrifying display of God's

---

53 Particularly, the Epic of Gilgamesh, the Epic of Atrahasis, and the story of Ziusudra. Sandra L. Richter, *The Epic of Eden: A Christian Entry into the Old Testament* (Downers Grove, IL: IVP Academic, 2008), 140–42.

wrath didn't fundamentally change the human heart—something greater would be required. The serpent crusher had not yet come (Gen. 3:15). Humanity would remain bent toward evil, but that wouldn't stop God from writing history with a redemptive arc.

We get a whiff of it when Noah stepped off the ark to build "an altar to the LORD" where he "offered burnt offerings" (Gen. 8:20). This "pleasing aroma" (Gen. 8:21) provoked God to commit to the preservation of humanity and the earth (see v. 22). Then God made the rainbow His tangible proof of His *hesed*—steadfast in love even if humanity wasn't (Gen. 9:11–17).

God's love remained a fire unquenched by the flood of His righteous wrath. And we—living, moving, and breathing today—are glad.

REFLECTION

Why is it important to notice both God's judgment and God's love in the story of Noah? How does noticing God's love in this story push back against the popular but misguided assumption that the God of the Old Testament is a God of wrath while the God of the New Testament is a God of mercy?

The City of Lovelessness

For they loved the glory that comes from man
more than the glory that comes from God.

JOHN 12:43

Remember God's blessing to "fill the earth" (Gen. 1:28), expanding Eden? Well, generations after Noah, humanity tried to prevent being "dispersed over the face of the whole earth" (Gen. 11:4). And thus began a tale of two cities.

Eden, "delight" in Hebrew, was the prototype temple of God, where heaven and earth were unified. It was likely on a mountain with rivers flowing out of it (Gen. 2:10–14; Ezek. 28:14, 16). It represented the city of God (the city of love), where His loving reign was embraced and enjoyed by a diverse yet unified creation. But the city of Babel was our ambition to preserve cultural uniformity. This trading of love—unity in diversity—for power—uniformity—is catastrophic commerce.

Native American author Mark Charles and Korean American author Soong-Chan Rah help us understand this by differentiating between Christianity, which is following the teachings and example of Christ, and the heresy of Christendom in which people seek an earthly Christian empire, often by coerced "conversions" and violence.[54] One seeks diverse relationships, while the other seeks power. One endures persecution, while the

---

54 Mark Charles and Soong-Chan Rah, *Unsettling Truths: The Ongoing, Dehumanizing Legacy of the Doctrine of Discovery* (Downers Grove, IL: InterVarsity Press, 2019), 14–23; 39–63.

other perpetrates it under the banner of becoming a "Christian" nation. One seeks faithfulness, while the other seeks dominance. Under the fourth-century idea of Christendom and in the Doctrine of Discovery, a papal bull issued in 1493, you'll find "justification" for so-called Christians leading the Crusades, the Spanish Inquisition, the colonization and enslavement of Africans, the genocide of indigenous peoples across the Americas, and further atrocities today—loving the earthly glory of cultural homogeneity "more than the glory that comes from God" (John 12:43).

Babel, later called Babylon, was a Mesopotamian major global power and a city symbolic of our institutional ambitions to dethrone God. Babylon represents corrupted humanity—our violent and oppressive appetite for dominance (Isa. 13:19; Rev. 17–18). It is the city of lovelessness.

Here, leadership is marked by sexual immorality, opulence, and slavery—the trafficking of "human souls" (Rev. 17:2; 18:3, 13). Here, cash is king (Matt. 26:14–16). Here, the oppressed cry with "no one to comfort them" (Eccl. 4:1). Here, religious life, zealous and festive though it may be, is marked by a disdain for the poor (Isa. 58:1–7), an unholy alliance with powerful leaders (John 19:15), and a neglect of social justice (Amos 5:21–24).

Do you know a place like this?

REFLECTION

How have you seen the city of lovelessness (Babel/Babylon) show up in your particular culture? How about in your experience of church or work?

The City of Love

Glorious things of you are spoken, O city of God.

PSALM 87:3

The tower at Babel was a serious construction endeavor. But God's issue wasn't and isn't with tall towers but rather tall ambitions for hegemony—the dominance of one culture or social group over all others. God *is* love—a diverse, unified, eternal community of Father, Son, and Spirit. His loving creation of humanity included His call to walk in His blessed will of cultural diversity, which would reflect His very nature. Like a parent redirecting his wandering toddler out of the busy road, God course-corrected humanity by diversifying their one language into many and "dispers[ing] them over the face of all the earth" (Gen. 11:9).[55]

At Babel, God continued what His loving plan was all along: a diverse humanity "from every nation, from all tribes and peoples and languages, standing before the throne" unified in their worship of God (Rev. 7:9–10). On the day of Pentecost, Jesus' first followers, who were Jews, would experience the Holy Spirit continuing this: God descending to a city of cultural uniformity (Jerusalem) and diversifying their language into many languages before sending them out to invite all the different cultures of the earth into God's diverse family (cf. Acts 2; Matt. 28:18–20; Acts 8:1, 4; Luke 4:25–32; Matt. 8:11).

---

55   The Hebrew word for "Babel" is "confusion" but is derived from a root word that means "to mix" (https://www.studylight.org/dictionaries/hbd/b/babel.html). At Babel, God mixed up (diversified) one human language into many, thus diversifying humanity's cultures.

At Babel, humanity missed the mark of God's blessed will of a dispersed and diverse humanity. To "miss the mark"—as in, missing the bull's-eye of a target—is what the word *sin* means. Yet God remained dedicated to the target of His story: a greater city, a New Jerusalem, filled with many languages, cultures, and colors, all united under Him. The city of love will triumph. And soon, we'll see how.

REFLECTION

How might God's unstoppable loving plan for the story of all creation speak to your biggest regrets in your life's story?

When I Consider the Darkness

I'm scared to raise you here, where
a reed basket can't deliver
an escape from the pain of your
    inheritance.
You're your Papi and me combined:
a Filipina, Puerto Rican, Jamaican,
    Colombian
a beautiful mix.
But what they'll see first
is your darkness
a sight for them of a less-than them
less than a man or woman.
Now, in our home you'll see this
we bear Christ's name above everything,
but this means
you'll wear not just one, but two targets
in this present darkness:
what they see immediately, then
what they see internally.
The first you can't deny, and shouldn't
the second they'll try but can't truly
    deny,
but it can be compromised . . .
so even in darkness tonight
my prayers plead for you
hidden in my dark belly
soon born to light
and this darkness
born dark
to little lights
born again (I pray):
dark to light
a dark child of light

hated by some
light children of darkness, yet
a light indestructible inside
can't be consumed by the present
    darkness.
A light indestructible inside
is more precious than your hated,
wonderfully made dark skin.

A light indestructible inside, my child,
can't be consumed by the present
darkness.

God's Love in
Your Story's Great Conflict

We all once lived in the passions of our flesh,
carrying out the desires of the body and the mind,
and were by nature children of wrath, like the rest of mankind.
But God, being rich in mercy, because of the great love
with which he loved us, even when we were dead in our trespasses,
made us alive together with Christ.

EPHESIANS 2:3–5

What was your story before God made you "alive together with Christ" (Eph. 2:5)? Let's review.

You were love-made by God to share in the love He has for His Son. You were made in His image as His royal representative, a partner, on earth to reflect His holy love in all you do. You were made with intrinsic worth and intricate design. But that's not all.

Because of your greatest-grandparents' rebellion against God, you were born with their sin-imprinted DNA. This means that within you is the propensity to disbelieve, ignore, and reject God's love through the way you think, speak, and act. God can't sweep sin under the rug and call it justice . . . or love. So yes, you were "by nature" ripe for His just wrath (Eph. 2:3). Still, God was patiently loving you, longing for you to turn away from your allegiance to evil and turn to Him instead (Ezek. 33:11). But that's not all.

God loved you sacrificially too. Though you were His enemy, He "gave his only Son" for you (John 3:16), about two thousand years before you took your first breath. God loved you, even before you loved Him (1 John 4:19)—as in, *way* before you loved Him.

This was your story before you found yourself on love's side of the battle line. Living in rejection of Love's calling was the great conflict of your story—really, *our* story. There's more adventure ahead, and with it, more exploration into the "breadth and length and height and depth" of God's love (Eph. 3:18). Care to come along?

REFLECTION

What's it like to read a short summary of the love God had for you *before* you trusted in Christ? Did any parts shock you, make you uncomfortable, delight you? Would you have summarized it like that?

A Loving Author, Developing Themes

You have kept count of my tossings; put my tears in your bottle.
Are they not in your book?

PSALM 56:8

W e've stepped into Eden, the setting of Scripture's story and the con-flict: humanity's rebellion. We've also been introduced to a few of our main characters: God, humanity, and the spiritual forces of evil. We've seen glimpses of the Author's intention, foreshadows of the story's coming climax, and a quick flash of its glorious resolution. We've witnessed some of Scripture's themes, like God's image, covenant, redemption, clothing, city, and temple. As the story continues, you'll notice more themes develop, like kingdom, rest, and marriage.

Would you believe that God has been developing themes in your indi-vidual story through main characters, important settings, and major events, too? This implies that your life does, in fact, have meaning—more than you can possibly imagine, but not less than you can explore. And as you explore your story—perhaps in therapy,[56] in your journal, or with friends and men-

---

56 I am not a licensed therapist, but I've benefited much from trauma therapy as well as story work counseling. So for more trauma-informed content from a biblical lens, I highly recommend the work of K. J. Ramsey, Adam Young, Dr. Monique Smith Gadson, and Dan Allender. I also highly recommend finding a licensed therapist or counselor if possible. Here's a place to start: https://adamyoungcounseling.com/referral-list/.

tors—maybe just maybe you'll find that some of your story's themes echo Scripture's. After all, they share the same Author.

As we move forward to meet our next main characters, be warned: each of them had major flaws, major setbacks and, no doubt, many tears. Doesn't it just remind us of our own stories? Thankfully, no tears are wasted in the stories God writes—Scripture's and yours. They're all kept in His bottle, recorded in His book—which, I'm happy to remind you, has a beautiful, redemptive arc.

REFLECTION

Are there any themes or images in Scripture's story that have impacted you? Why do you think that particular theme/image/story struck a chord with you?

How have you seen God's love shine through your life's story so far? What might the theme/image/story from Scripture that impacted you in your answer above have to do with a theme in your own story?

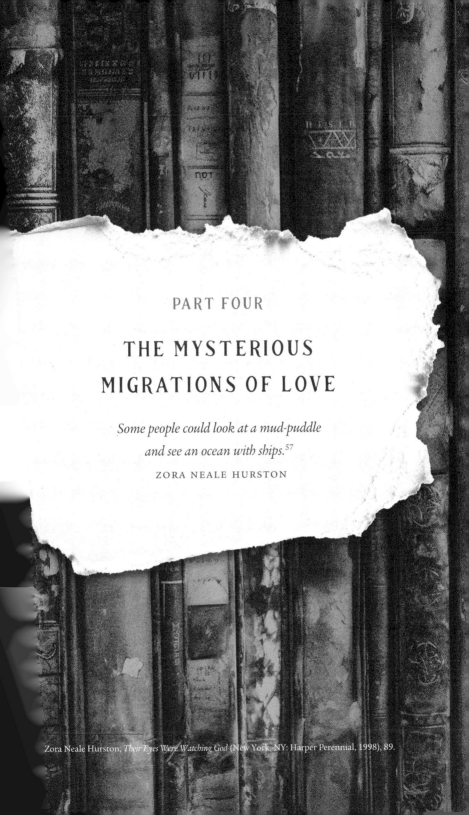

PART FOUR

THE MYSTERIOUS MIGRATIONS OF LOVE

*Some people could look at a mud-puddle
and see an ocean with ships.*[57]

ZORA NEALE HURSTON

Zora Neale Hurston, *Their Eyes Were Watching God* (New York, NY: Harper Perennial, 1998), 89.

Cuando hace calor[58]

Calor, calor, calor
cuando hace calor
I'm transported to your back porch
whiffs of tangerines, grapefruits,
oranges
echoes of cousins
squealing "hide and seek!"
you'd scold us if we forgot to kiss
    your cheek
is this breeze in my hair
the same air from then?
Did it travel from the Caribbean
like you did back when
your Mami died and you were just
    a kid?
You came from the warmth
to the streets of the North
back and forth—PR, New York.
You told me once,
"I was just . . . there.
I never felt important."

Shouts and sirens, no silence
unheard in Manhattan's masses
save for peace in the pews
of the Catholic Masses
you'd take yourself to.
Did you imagine
you'd forever feel invisible, little?

Did you know good stories
never stop in the middle?
By the end
the hospice could barely fit us all in that
        room
singing *alabanzas* for the gift of you.

You were an orphan of sorts
who made a home.
48 Winding Ridge was your throne.

The best *sueñitos* are intangible.
Legacies of love
left to spread.
Never dead.

---

58 This piece is a poem-in-conversation with the song "Paciencia y Fe" by Lin-Manuel Miranda (sung by Olga Merediz) in the film *In the Heights* (2021). A poem-in-conversation is meant to connect one piece of literature or art (in this case, a song by Lin-Manuel Miranda) to another (my poem). It's a way of honoring a piece of literature that strongly inspired an original piece. The poem itself is my own creation.

In the Land of Lovelessness, Love Calls

It is he who remembered us in our low estate,
for his steadfast love endures forever.

PSALM 136:23

I n the ashes of defeat, Adam and Eve hear the promise of a conquering offspring (Gen. 3:15). Drenched by the certain PTSD of witnessing the world around him drown, Noah hears the promise of earth's preservation and a new creation (Gen. 8:21–9:17). And now, after humanity is diversified and spread across the earth (Gen. 11:1–9), the lineage of Seth, a.k.a. "team serpent crusher," progresses into the lineage of Noah's son Shem, which leads us to a man named Abram, later renamed Abraham.

Abram is called by God to leave his hometown with the promise of a new home (Gen. 12:1). He's called to leave his security and identity—his "father's house"—with the promise of a new identity, a name that is "great" (Gen. 12:1–2). He's called to leave his gods, which he served for over seventy years (Josh. 24:2), to follow after the one true God. He's called to be the covenant representative through which "all the families of the earth shall be blessed" (Gen. 12:3).

The word "curse" is repeated five times throughout mankind's rebellion in Genesis 3–11.[59] But now the word "bless" is repeated five times in

---

59 Genesis 3:14, 17; 4:11; 5:29; 8:21.

Genesis 12:1–3. What could this mean? Through Abram, God would continue to reverse earth's curse. Abram is called *by* the love of God, *to* the love of God, *for the global embrace of* the love of God (Gen. 12:3; Rev. 7:9). The great story of redemption continues!

Remember Babylon, the city of lovelessness? God chose Abram, a man of Ur in Babylonia—the state that also contained the city of Babylon. Abram's pedigree wasn't strong. His list of references didn't hold up. He was from Babylonia. Yet here goes God: "I will bless you" (Gen. 12:2). Do you think where you come from is any hindrance to the love of God?

Reflection

> What feelings pop up when you think about where you're from: your hometown, family of origin, socioeconomic class, something else? What are the aspects of your life that make you feel inferior to others? What type of person/people/culture(s) do you sometimes feel superior to? Why?

Beloved Migrants

By faith Abraham obeyed when he was called to go
out to a place that he was to receive as an inheritance.
And he went out, not knowing where he was going.
By faith he went to live in the land of promise, as in a foreign land,
living in tents with Isaac and Jacob, heirs with him of the same promise.
For he was looking forward to the city that has foundations,
whose designer and builder is God.

HEBREWS 11:8–10

Abram was promised Canaan, but he lived the rest of his life as a migrant. "They set out for the land of Canaan, and they arrived there" (Gen. 12:5 NIV). But they didn't get to stay. Abram and Sarai's family would have to endure many migrations before their descendants would finally settle in this Promised Land.

Their descendants would later declare, "A wandering Aramean was my father," as they offered sacrifices of firstfruits in the Promised Land—remembering those mysterious migrations God required before His promise of land was fulfilled (Deut. 26:5). Within the regular worship practices of Israel would be an embedded care for migrants, reminding them of God's loving care for them through their nomadic history (Deut. 10:18–19; 26:12–15).

Why would God have Abram walk the Promised Land, then make him and his descendants migrants—sojourners passing through famine, oppressive governments, and family strife? Could it be that through Abram and Sarai, who "acknowledged that they were strangers and exiles on the earth" (Heb. 11:13), God was teaching us something about our status in Christ "as sojourners and exiles" on this earth (1 Peter 2:11)? That to be the "beloved" of God means seeking "a better country, that is, a heavenly one" (Heb. 11:16)?

Could it be that Love calls us into a blessing that is birthed *through* paths of uncertainty, pain, and mystery?

REFLECTION

Why do you think God called the families of promise (Abraham, Isaac, Jacob, Joseph, and Moses, for example) into the struggles of migration? Why would God Himself become a refugee (Matt. 2)? What do you think we as Christ followers can learn from the voices and stories of refugees, asylum seekers, migrants, and immigrants?[60]

When has a life transition taught you something about God's steadfast love?

---

60 If you haven't given this much thought before, I recommend starting with Karen Gonzalez's book *Beyond Welcome: Centering Immigrants in Our Christian Response to Immigration* (Ada, MI: Brazos Press, 2022). Another book for your consideration: *Seeking Refuge: On the Shores of the Global Refugee Crisis* (Chicago, IL: Moody Publishers, 2016) by Stephan Bauman, Matthew Soerens, and Dr. Issam Smeir.

Welcome to the Faith

at 16. and

back then,

I'd have run through a rod

for my God.

brand new believer

Welcome, Quina.

you'll never be the same.

and I wasn't.

but, then again,

back then,

I saw no face

to mirror

my emotional conflictedness

at my parents' split

just months

after I prayed

my first true "Amen."

back when,

I didn't know

I should maybe mention

home was swallowing me whole

and the only touch

that seemed safe

touched me in ways

that shoveled me

under my shame

bearing Your name

but sneaking hands

where they shouldn't be

welcome to the faith, welcome to secrecy.

back then,

You were new to me

yet

You were my everything.

I knew to follow meant

carrying cross, yet

staring at addiction's grimace—

the way it makes

the finest face

shrivel and sink

deflating the ability to dream—

at 17,

I admit, I didn't expect that.

back when,

I'd cringe in class

as kids laughed and rapped

about crack

cocaine, like it didn't just disintegrate

everything around me

like it wasn't the enemy

no, back then,

I thought maybe this was it

maybe this was Your plan for me, my

purpose

to never get out, so . . . I quit

(to my forever-chagrin,

it seems)

volleyball dreams, my student-athlete

trajectory

back when,

my high school coach,

(who'd known a bit about my home)

for some reason

made it his mission

to torment me

all season, antagonizing

my newfound faith.
then pulled me aside
to tell me a lie
I'd spend the rest of my life
trying not to believe
(but I believed it then)
he drew a chart on a paper,
pointed to its peak and said,
"this is you now. almost 18.
this is the best you'll ever be.
it's only downhill from here."
back when,
I'd already seen
my friend die
my mentor die
my life
tear at the seams.
back then,
I didn't know this was all called
trauma
that my brain would
black out memories
my body would keep
my nightmares would
later remind me
of
back when,
I began
this great migration
away from hoping in my own
fleeting sense of success
to hoping in the resurrection
yes, back then
my childhood experienced
its own sort of death,

welcomed to the faith
with pain I still feel today
but, back then,

I remember, I refuse to forget
yes, I refuse to forget:
I'd lay my head on the pillow
and pray to this Jesus
I'd found myself
in love with, this
Jesus, who, I knew,
had changed me
was changing me within
and, back then,
You gave me a vision
in the screaming silence
of my loneliness:
    there You were, holding me
    with scarred hands, you'd rock me
    in the night
    'til finally, I'd
    fall asleep.

Welcomed to the faith,
I've never been the same.

A Certain Love

When the sun had gone down and it was dark, behold,
a smoking fire pot and a flaming torch passed between these pieces.

GENESIS 15:17

God promised Abram would become a "great nation" (Gen. 12:2) and a blessing for "all the families of the earth" (Gen. 12:3). A bit of a tall order—enough for Abram to doubt. It had been almost a decade since he first heard God's promise, and he was no closer to becoming a great nation than the sun was to high-fiving the moon. So when God reiterated His promises, Abram had some questions: "What will you give me, for I continue childless . . . how am I to know that I shall possess [Canaan]?" (Gen. 15:2, 8).

As Abram's faith wavered, God displayed the certainty of His promise through a covenant ceremony, which would have been very familiar to Abram—but rather strange to most of us today. Back in Abram's day, "cutting" a covenant sometimes included cutting animals in half and walking between them with your covenant partner. This symbolized that if you were to break your covenant commitments, then your flesh, too, should be torn. And if your covenant partner were to break covenant, then he should be the one torn apart like those animals. Covenant-keeping (*hesed*) was kind of a big deal.

Yet it is only God—represented by "a smoking fire pot and a flaming torch" (Gen. 15:17)—who passes between the torn animals. (This is the part when you gasp.) Why didn't God have Abram pass through the animals, too? He was communicating something profound: if God were to break His covenant promises, He would be as these torn animals—punished to death. But if Abram and his descendants were to break their covenant commitments, their flesh *wouldn't* be torn. God's would.

This certain love persevered through centuries of covenant breaking by Abraham's descendants, until God Himself tore bread, reminiscent of those torn animals, and proclaimed, "this is my body" (Matt. 26:26).

REFLECTION

By establishing this covenant, God put His own character on the line. What difference does it make to know that God connects your perseverance in the faith to His own reputation of certain love (Ps. 25:7; 44:26)?

Solid Love for a Shaky Faith

You will show faithfulness to Jacob and steadfast love to Abraham,
as you have sworn to our fathers from the days of old.

MICAH 7:20

The Abrahamic covenant, which is what we talked about yesterday, teaches us that God's love for His children is certain. His is a "sure love" (Isa. 55:3), unwavering and unthwarted by our moments of doubt, sin, and weakness.

When God promised Abram countless offspring, Genesis 15:6 tells us "he believed the LORD, and he counted it to him as righteousness." But Abram's doubts are expressed in Genesis 15, and they're acted out in conjunction with Sarai's doubts in Genesis 16. Sarai gave her Egyptian slave, Hagar, as another wife for Abram in hopes that she might bear a child. So he literally impregnated a servant in hopes of achieving what God had promised would come through his wife. This caused Hagar to be put in an impossible situation of near-destitution and disgrace.

Incredibly, God stepped in to bless and protect Hagar and her son Ishmael, despite the abuse and failure of the family of promise (Gen. 16; 21:8–21). Notice how much God spoke to Hagar in comparison to Sarai (Gen. 16, 21). Notice how God calls Hagar by name (Gen. 16:8; 21:17), and how Hagar becomes the first person in Scripture's story to name God (*El-Roi*: "the God who sees," or "You are a God who sees me" in Gen. 16:13). God's love would not be boxed in by His people's failures to love. His love would even extend beyond His covenant people who failed to truly *see* the vulnerable around them.

Abraham and Sarah didn't pass every test of faith (Gen. 12:10–20; 16:1–6; 17:17–18; 20:1–2), but their faith grew stronger over the years as they witnessed God's persistent, rock-solid love. Their doubts were not the final word in their story (Heb. 11:11–12).

REFLECTION

How might this motivate you to move toward God with your questions, frustrations, and doubts?

Little one, big heart
(Portrait of Jael, age 6)

When I was about your age
I lay with my mom on the couch
and remember so clearly
even to my nerve endings
how her belly would rise and sink
and I'd try to breathe
in sync with her, but in truth
her breaths were bigger.
and the best part
of lying on her chest
was acknowledging that fact.
and the subsequent
surrender: held
in a safe embrace.

At age six you endured more than
    I'd prefer.
I saw you thrive
with what we thought were
lifelong friends, from your
neighborhood, church, kindergarten, then
plucked you out to live in a place
that felt more of a vacation than
a space to stay—so far from them.

You lost lots
little one, big heart
especially because
you tend to love so hard.
and though I know that pang
that rawness
I'd never wish it

on you, or wish
to be the cause of it.

Resilient. Yep, that's you.
But you carry grief, too.

And you're allowed to.
You're allowed to be mad
you can't have siblings
you can't always play with me
because of my fatigue
you don't hear from some
of your old best friends
you suffer for "Mommy's disease."
This year you learned
you had that
permission to feel angry
for these things, to feel grief
to express it. and for me:
same.

Into little pieces the heart breaks
only to expand
when held, again and again,
in a safe embrace.

And in this way, your childlike faith
grew some ridges and depth.
At age 6, you held space
for hard feelings
learned how to pray in
the language of lament
AND (and it's a big "and,"
little one, big heart)
you developed a gradual openness

to a new start, trying new things—
no training wheels, skateboarding,
roller-skating, new friends.
you've been
the light
that's reminded me
to hope
to treasure the tiniest things
to laugh
to choose softness when
the heart erodes or hardens
to pay attention
to answered prayers
to study you
to study me, too—because

the best thing I can do for you
little one, big heart
is to see to
the mending of
my own wounds
so you
can know
breath after breath
yours little, mine big
that sweet surrender
to a safe embrace
you and God, me and you

when you lie down
with me, too.

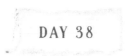
A Tested Love

After these things God tested Abraham and said to him,
"Abraham!" And he said, "Here I am."
He said, "Take your son, your only son Isaac, whom you love,
and go to the land of Moriah, and offer him there as a burnt offering
on one of the mountains of which I shall tell you."

GENESIS 22:1–2

Finally: the very first explicit mention of "love" in the biblical narrative! But surprisingly, the scene isn't a marriage ceremony or a birth. It's an ominous landscape of looming death. Wasn't the God of Abraham different from those ancient Near Eastern gods who required child sacrifices?

Abraham is tested by God so the validity of his faith could shine through his radical obedience (James 2:21–23; 1 Peter 1:6–7). After all, can faith claim validity if left untested? Can't we say the same thing about love? Abraham's test was a test of love. Who would he love more: his son or his God? Abraham's *hesed* was being tested. But so was God's.

God's love is a tested love, tried and true. But now Isaac
the child of promise (cf. Matt. 1:1),
carried wood for the sacrifice on his back (cf. John 19:17),
up a hill (cf. Mark 15:22),
to die at the hands of his father (cf. Rom. 8:32).

Now his father's knife gleamed in the morning sun, suspended in midair. And now we behold the love of God, proven and prototyped. God pauses the terrifying scene with a word and a substitute for the sacrifice: "a ram, caught in a thicket by his horns" (Gen. 22:13).

Abraham witnessed something we see more clearly today (John 8:56). God Himself would provide a sacrifice to suffer in our place for our sins—"the Lamb of God, who takes away the sin of the world" (John 1:29). And that Lamb of God would be none other than His Son: His "only Son" (John 3:16), His "beloved Son" (Matt. 17:5). What God did *not* require of Abraham He *would* require of Himself: He "did not spare his own Son but gave him up for us all" (Rom. 8:32).

Has there ever been a love more tested?

REFLECTION

How has God's love been tested and proven in your life so far?

A Love We Can't Finagle

And Jacob said,
"O God of my father Abraham and God of my father Isaac . . .
I am not worthy of the least of all the deeds of steadfast love
and all the faithfulness that you have shown to your servant."

GENESIS 32:9–10

Abraham's grandson was a downright deceiver. Literally, that was his name: Jacob means "he cheats" (Gen. 25:24–26).[61] He tricked his older twin, Esau, out of his birthright (Gen. 25:29–34), and his nearly blind father, Isaac, into giving him the blessing reserved for his firstborn son (Gen. 27). Even when God proclaimed his covenant promise to him, Jacob responded with something more like a business proposition than humble faith (Gen. 28:10–22). Jacob was a schemer. He connived his way to success.

That is, until God lovingly humbled him through a twenty-year-long exile to Paddan-aram where he was consistently tricked by his uncle Laban (Gen. 29–31). What happens when a schemer meets his match? He begins to acknowledge God's gracious presence is the only thing that has kept him afloat (Gen. 31:41–42). He begins to realize God's kindness is the kind that's unmerited, something he can't finagle, or manipulate, his way into receiving.

But when Jacob escapes his deceiving uncle to return home as God commanded (Gen. 31:3), the consequences of his past treachery haunt him. He's told that Esau, who had previously expressed plans to kill Jacob, is on

---

61   Or "he grasps," "he takes by the heel," or "deceiver."

his way toward him with "four hundred men" (Gen. 32:6)—a certain sign of attack. After decades of duplicity, desperate Jacob prays today's passage.

When God then let Jacob wrestle with him (and even win), Jacob left with a broken hip and a changed identity. No longer was he "Jacob the cheater"; he was now Israel, the one who had "striven with God and with men, and [had] prevailed" (Gen. 32:28). The one whose limp would help him lean on the steadfast love of God. The one who triumphed by letting go of his deceptive scheming and refusing to let go of God.

REFLECTION

What are some ways you try to finagle—scheme, connive, grasp—your way into God's love? (Perhaps through ministry or trying to make up for certain sins by serving God instead of confessing your sin and trusting in His ready forgiveness. Perhaps you assume God owes you certain blessings because of your obedience.) How does it land on you when you hear that God's love cannot be manipulated, but instead is freely given and unearned? Can you recall a time when God allowed you to face a difficulty so great that you could only rely on Him?

DAY 40

Love's Chorus

But the LORD was with Joseph and showed him steadfast love.

GENESIS 39:21

There's a chorus in the life of Jacob's favorite son, Joseph. If you listen closely you'll hear it.

You probably know his story. It foreshadows our Savior's:

After receiving prophetic dreams of royalty, Joseph told his **jealous older brothers** (cf. John 10:30–39),

who then **conspired to kill him** (cf. Matt. 12:14; John 1:11).

Instead, they "make a killing off of him"[62] by **selling him** into slavery in Egypt (cf. Matt. 26:14–16).

Despite his enslavement, Joseph became highly valued in the house of Potiphar, an officer of Pharaoh. But soon he became devalued— objectified by Potiphar's wife who punished Joseph's integrity with a **false accusation** (cf. Matt. 26:59–60).

While in prison for three years, he was **forgotten and abandoned** by a prisoner friend who had promised to advocate for Joseph once he got out (cf. Matt. 26:31–35).

---

62 John Onwuchekwa, "Getting Past Our Past," The Front Porch National Conference 2019, https://www.youtube.com/watch?v=WLjS7p_4Lho, at 10:26.

121

But when Joseph successfully interpreted Pharaoh's dreams, **he was exalted, seated at the right hand of the king** (cf. Mark 16:19; Acts 5:31).

God took Joseph through some of the worst injustices a person could endure. But if Joseph's life had a soundtrack, you'd hear a steady chorus throughout the euphony *and* the cacophony: "the LORD was with him, showing him steadfast love" (see Gen. 39:2, 3, 21, 23). In the pit of betrayal, in the hands of traffickers, in the face of false accusation, in the prison of abandonment, *and* in his success—the Lord was with him.

The chorus in Joseph's life was God's ever-present love—the same chorus echoing through your life's soundtrack (Rom. 8:38–39).

REFLECTION

Perhaps you're currently in the pit of betrayal or the prison of abandonment. How might God's chorus of overriding love in Joseph's story comfort you as your story still develops?

An Overriding Love

His brothers also came and fell down before him and said,
"Behold, we are your servants." But Joseph said to them,
"Do not fear, for am I in the place of God?
As for you, you meant evil against me, but God meant it for good,
to bring it about that many people should be kept alive, as they are today."

GENESIS 50:18–20

G od, in His love, used the unthinkable actions of Joseph's brothers to save the people in the land of Canaan from famine. God's loving plan didn't justify their sin but overcame it.

God's steadfast love (*hesed*) couldn't be thwarted by gross injustice. His promise to Eve (Gen. 3:15) and to Abraham (Gen. 12:1–3) couldn't be snuffed out by the evil intentions of people—even God's own people. God's love is an overriding kind of love, and it can never be outplayed by Satan's crafty tactics. It is a sovereign love, coming out on top despite, and even *through*, humanity's wicked deeds (Acts 2:23).

Joseph's words of forgiveness toward his brothers is the message of the book of Genesis and, really, the whole Bible: "As for you, you meant evil against me, but God meant it for good, to bring it about that many people should be kept alive, as they are today" (Gen. 50:20).

Through rejected Joseph's providential pain,
Israel was saved;[63]
and through Christ's,
the whole world. (1 John 2:2)

It's hard to read Joseph's story and not see in it the story of the African American church—a people stolen and separated from their families, trafficked, raped, forced into free labor, falsely accused of numerous crimes, and villainized by people who claimed to know and love God. And yet, through unspeakable injustices, God has raised up generations of Black Christians who have advanced the kingdom of God. The existence and survival of the Black church is evidence of God's overriding love.

REFLECTION

What do you know of the history of the Black Christian church? What do you think you might learn from the African-American experience and other marginalized Christian traditions?[64]

---

63 Quina Aragon, "Listen and Live," https://www.youtube.com/watch?v=U5wYDSio4eA&t=516s.

64 Might I recommend starting with the speech "Learning from the African-American Church Experience" by K. A. Ellis (Director of the Edmiston Center)? https://www.youtube.com/watch?v=OMyRUSK9DdA. You will also be blessed to hear Tyler Burn's message "The Gift of the Black Christian Experience" (Q Ideas), https://www.youtube.com/watch?v=jbZpEk-VU2U. Another resource is Tony Evans's *A Survey of the Black Church in America*, especially chapter 5, "The Uniqueness of the Black Church" (Chicago, IL: Moody Publishers, 2024).

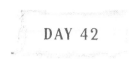

What About the Matriarchs?

The Lord gives the word;
the women who announce the news are a great host.

PSALM 68:11

It would be more than unfortunate if we left this section on what's often called "the patriarchal age" of the Bible with the assumption that God primarily or preferably works in and through the lives of men rather than women.

Indeed, much of the Bible's setting was in a society that was patriarchal, meaning the family was structured around the oldest male. It was also patrilineal, in that ancestral descent and tribal affiliation were traced through the male line. And it was patrilocal, meaning family living spaces were designed around the oldest male.[65] But God, through His works and words, often critiqued aspects of this society, including its treatment of women—just as His Word critiques aspects of our modern society.

Elyse Fitzpatrick and Eric Schumacher remind us:

When God first proclaimed the Gospel, he promised deliverance through the offspring of the woman (Genesis 3:15). The deliverer will come through her. This promise teaches us to "watch the woman" as the storyline unfolds so that we see the Redeemer when he arrives. In looking for, noticing, and celebrating women in the storyline of the

---

65 Sandra L. Richter, *The Epic of Eden: A Christian Entry into the Old Testament* (Downers Grove, IL: IVP Academic, 2008), 25–38.

Bible, we are not sliding down a slippery slope of liberalism, about to careen off a cliff into all-out goddess worship. Looking for, noticing, and celebrating women in the storyline of the Bible is climbing the ladder of careful Bible interpretation, seeing the rungs that the Author put in place, and stepping accordingly.[66]

God reconnects with sinful humanity through covenants with Noah, Abraham, Moses, David, and finally, through His own Son. But this global work of new creation could not (and cannot) happen apart from the faith of women: Eve's faith despite her initial failure (Gen. 3:15; 4:25–26), Sarah's faith despite her fertility struggles (Heb. 11:11), Hagar's faith despite her enslavement and abuse (Gen. 16; 21), and Tamar's faith despite her father-in-law's wickedness (Gen. 38). And these are just some of the women—the matriarchs, if you will—mentioned in Scripture's story up to this point! Like the patriarchs—Abraham, Isaac, and Jacob—these women were flawed but faithful.

The oppression of women—about which Scripture does not turn a blind eye (Gen. 34; 2 Sam. 13)—is a direct result of the rebellion of mankind in the Garden of Eden (Gen. 3:16). But the promised Seed of Eve was coming. He would be born of a woman, and His life would be marked by His inclusion, healing, and commissioning of women—even women of shady reputation. So as you read through the story of Scripture, notice God's love for women. It might just shock you, move you, and make you love Him even more.

REFLECTION

What are some ways you have noticed women not being valued in Christian community? What are some ways you've noticed the opposite?

How might intentionally noticing women in Scripture help you develop a more robust appreciation of God's inclusion of women in His kingdom agenda?

---

66 Elyse Fitzpatrick and Eric Schumacher, *Worthy: Celebrating the Value of Women* (Bloomington, MN: Bethany House Publishers, 2020), 19–20.

What's a Woman Worth?[67]

"Happy is he whose children are males,
and woe to him whose children are
females."[68]
a quote from rabbis of old
but if you look close, you know
this sentiment isn't frozen in the past
in fact, I see it
an expecting father bows his head in
defeat
at the sight of pink confetti
a rape victim is shamed
for ruining the reputation of an "otherwise standup guy"
a woman works for half the price
a man would achieve
the words "feminist" and "liberal"
are wielded as weapons against
those who'd dare speak of misogyny . . .
in the church.

It makes me wonder, what's a woman
worth?
looked for it in lyrics and sermons
and thought,
"She's a vice, a vixen, a problem to solve."
so I dug deeper, sought the song first sung
the very first words
straight out of Adam's tongue:
"This at last is bone of my bones
and flesh of my flesh;

she shall be called Woman,
because she was taken out of Man."
The first song in Scripture proclaims a
woman's worth.
she's same of same, fully human
made in God's image, but
it's likely you already knew this.

No need to tell you
that while the first sin was eating
forbidden fruit
the second was a woman's abuse
from the balladeer's tongue would come
an excuse, accusing the woman he once
sung of
"The woman whom *you*
gave to be with me
she gave me fruit of the tree,
and I ate."

Generations later still rings the same
refrain:
"Well, if she hadn't worn that . . ."
"If she hadn't talked back . . ."
"If she dare speak or lead . . ."
ah, but we don't want to talk about that.

See, we see redemptive history
as a series of men and the ways God
used them
but the first gospel proclamation

---

67 Quina Aragon, "What's a Woman Worth?," https://youtu.be/GrS9zDsgr_o.
68 Elyse Fitzpatrick and Eric Schumacher, *Worthy: Celebrating the Value of Women* (Bloomington, MN: Bethany House Publishers, 2020), 291.

requires us to "watch the woman"
through whom would come
the serpent-crushing seed
so (it just seems)
Satan's special hatred is reserved
for women with whom he's at enmity.
But is a woman's worth unorthodox to
God?

Ask Eve who believed Genesis 3:15
trace her faith
through a long line of ladies leading
   straight
      to Mary's Magnificat
the first hymn of the New Covenant
   people of God.
Ask the women who followed the Christ
the marginalized and stigmatized
the barren and bereaved
the mistreated and abused, they drew
near to the Son of Man who would
   choose
to wash feet with all that authority.
It seems they finally found One
who was despised and rejected by men,
acquainted with grief . . . like them.
When he rose from the dead
he spoke first to the women
commissioned them to tell the men
the good news
but they were shooed away (like today)
unworthy of proclaiming God's Word
to the ears of men, which apparently
couldn't possibly learn from them.

Except, that's not how Jesus saw it
that's not how Paul taught it
the Great Commission made
every type of woman
acclaimed or not, a herald of the gospel
mom or not, a mother of many disciples
wife or not, the Bride of Christ.
all in all, a worthy child of God.

What's a woman worth, then?
No less than
His life,
His death,
His resurrection.

A Loving Author, Mysterious Paths

All the paths of the LORD *are steadfast love and faithfulness,*
for those who keep his covenant and his testimonies.

PSALM 25:10

In Yaa Gyasi's brilliant historical novel *Homegoing*, the story of Effia and Esi, Ghanaian half-sisters, is told through tracing their descendants generation by generation.[69] The narrative lines of these two lineages, impacted by the transatlantic slave trade, are complex—equally devastating and beautiful. The themes of fire (Effia's lineage) and water (Esi's lineage) develop through eight generations until they converge as the sisters' descendants return home together.

The Bible tells a story—the ultimate story—a bit like this.

The great story of new creation is one in which God brings us home to a greater Eden, the New Jerusalem (Rev. 21), and it begins with a call to leave home (Gen. 12:1-3). In these mysterious migrations ordained by Love, Abraham faced famine (Gen. 12), war (Gen. 14), familial strife (Gen. 16; 21), failed pregnancies (Gen. 18), and his own wavering faith and unwise decisions (Gen. 12; 16; 20). His son Isaac and grandson Jacob faced similar struggles. Their family of origin shaped them more than they may have realized.

"One's family of origin—the family one grew up in, as opposed to the

---

69   Yaa Gyasi, *Homegoing* (New York, NY: Knopf, 2016).

people one currently lives with—is the place that people typically learn to become who they are. From the family of origin a person learns how to communicate, process emotions, and get needs met. People also learn many of their values and beliefs from their families."[70] As it's said: "Jesus might live in your heart, but Grandpa lives in your bones."[71] The apple doesn't fall far from the tree; but God can birth nutrition from rotten things. Your family of origin contains narratives, traumas, and values that play a huge role in your story. Engaging this can be raw, bewildering work. Yet all—even the mysterious—paths of God "are steadfast love and faithfulness" (Ps. 25:10).

The stories of Abraham's family tree are complex—equally devastating and beautiful. Yet God's love holds the story together until it reaches its climax in Abraham's ultimate offspring, "who is Christ" (Gal. 3:16; cf. Gen. 22:18). Your mystifying past, perplexing present, and mysterious future are held together by the steadfast love of an Author whose specialty, I'm happy to remind you, is writing with a redemptive arc.

REFLECTION

What are some words you might use to describe your family of origin (e.g., the role you played in your family, the unspoken rules, the communication styles, how you were shaped to respond to authority or conflict, etc.)? What are some of the most confusing paths you've walked in life so far? What aspects of your life seem mysterious to you? What are some aspects of your story that still seem "in the dark"—not yet greatly affected by Scripture's story of God's great love?

---

70 "Family of Origin Issues," GoodTherapy, https://www.goodtherapy.org/learn-about-therapy/issues/family-of-origin-issues.

71 Rich Villodas, *The Deeply Formed Life: Five Transformative Values to Root Us in the Way of Jesus* (Colorado Springs, CO: WaterBrook, 2020), 112.

to remember redemptively: my dream

to: younger me
come sit with me
  I'll hold your
  dimpled hand
  and wait
  with patience
  'til you're ready
  for the embrace
  of a safe adult.

  I'll weep with you
  that, yes,
  the world's a big, scary place
  but home should've never
  been the same.

  I'll sit with you in the silence
  I'll hold the punching pad
  while you express your rage
  to my welcoming face

Together, by grace,
we'll see slowly
      body and mind
         reconciling
           like all things, in Him.

to: Jesus
come hold me
   please, grant my soul some rest
   take my lifetime of encaged rage

and sit with me
at the tomb of my dreams
'til sadness is swallowed
into an eternity of redemption.
sing over my story
a song of lament
rock me in the night
'til I sleep, 'til I forget
the pain of my father's house
      make me a Mannasah
      make me an Ephraim[72]
wrap me in your wounded hands
while I hold the child within.
you hold us both, for
underneath are
the everlasting arms[73]
the scarred hands,
resurrected.

---

72 "Joseph called the name of the firstborn Manasseh. 'For,' he said, 'God has made me forget all my hardship and all my father's house.' The name of the second he called Ephraim, 'For God has made me fruitful in the land of my affliction'" (Gen. 41:51-52).
73 "The eternal God is your dwelling place, and underneath are the everlasting arms" (Deut. 33:27).

131

PART FIVE

LOVE'S RESCUE AND RULE, YOUR PROGRESSING PLOT

No one forgets that they were once captive,
even if they are now free.[74]

AKUA IN YAA GYASI, *HOMEGOING*

Yaa Gyasi, *Homegoing* (New York: Knopf, 2016), Kindle, 242.

Love Empathizes

Hear my voice according to your steadfast love;
O LORD, according to your justice give me life.

PSALM 119:49

God had promised Abraham that his descendants would be sojourners and servants, afflicted for four hundred years before God would
deliver them (Gen. 15:13–14; cf. 48:21; 50:24). But who could've anticipated
the severity of brutality they'd face in Egypt once a new pharaoh took the
throne? Xenophobic accusations: "Behold, the people of Israel are too
many and too mighty for us. . . . They are lazy." (See Ex. 1:8–10; 5:8–9 NIV.)
Countless baby boys murdered—their blood crying out from the Nile (Ex.
1:22). Inhumane slavery: "the Egyptians worked them ruthlessly" (Ex. 1:14
NIV). Generations of abuse with no end in sight. But notice the progression
of verbs in Exodus 2:24–25:

> "God heard" their cries for rescue, their groanings (cf. Rom. 8:23–27).
> "God remembered" His covenant promises to Abraham (cf. Ps. 105:42).
> "God saw" His people—their victimization, their pain.
> "God knew."

Throughout Scripture's story, you'll find a pattern of God seeing a situation, feeling a particular emotion in reaction to that situation, and then
acting. God's all-knowing, all-seeing, unchanging, sovereign nature doesn't
stop Him from reacting to earth's affairs with real emotion. Jesus, the Son

of God, would later embody this progression when "he *saw* a great crowd, and he *had compassion* on them and *healed* their sick" (Matt. 14:14, emphasis mine; also see Matt. 9:36; Luke 15:20; John 11:32–35).

Love leans into pain with something more than a word to "look at the bright side." It doesn't look away from the ugly realities of others' experiences. Love feels. It empathizes with the afflicted, and then seeks to make right what's been made wrong for *all* who are oppressed (Deut. 7:8; Ps. 103:6).

REFLECTION

How might God's compassionate attention to the enslaved Israelites' groanings help you better acknowledge, validate, and give yourself permission to feel your own emotions, especially the hard ones? How might God's see-feel-act progression better inform your treatment of other people's painful circumstances and emotions?

DAY 45

Love Looks Like Freedom

The LORD works righteousness and justice for all who are oppressed.
He made known his ways to Moses, his acts to the people of Israel.

PSALM 103:6-7

God made Himself known to Moses—a boy affected by unjust family separations, a man whose misguided attempts at justice led him to murder, a wanderer dwelling far from his hometown. To this man, the God of Abraham appeared in an unconsumed, fiery bush, revealing His very name: "I AM WHO I AM"—Yahweh (Ex. 3:14). The eternal, self-sufficient God who absolutely exists—not just one among the so-called gods of Egypt.[75] Then, through nine plagues, "I AM" shut the mouths of Egypt's false gods. But it was the tenth that finally did Pharaoh in. Death spread to every first-born in Egypt, including Pharaoh's son, but not including the homes of the Hebrews who covered their doorposts with the blood of innocent lambs. Redemption smelled like blood. On that first Passover night, God thrust His people out from the house of slavery with the spoils of their oppressors (Ex. 12:35–36).

When Pharaoh made a last-ditch effort to re-enslave God's liberated people, God miraculously delivered them through the Red Sea. The waters they passed through to salvation were the same waters the Egyptians faced in their damnation. Remember: judgment and salvation are almost always coupled in Scripture. God crushed their evil enemy, and so they sang on

---

75 Quina Aragon, "Listen and Live (Spoken Word Short Film)," https://youtu.be/U5wYDSio4eA.

that beach shore: "You have led in your steadfast love the people whom you have redeemed" (Ex. 15:13).

Had the world ever heard of a god who chose to side with an enslaved people group of no acclaim? Had a god ever been associated with such weakness? Had a god ever been so proud to call the oppressed his "firstborn son" (Ex. 4:22)? What kind of love is this? The kind that keeps its promises, that moves toward the victimized, that is unrivaled by global superpowers. The kind that looks like freedom. Why else do you think American slave owners, and their British counterparts, removed major parts of the Bible, like Exodus?[76]

The narrative arc of Scripture bends toward freedom. It is, in fact, a major theme of the Bible's story. "The LORD works righteousness and justice for all who are oppressed" (Ps. 103:6; cf. Luke 4:18). From the outset, God made it clear: He intended spiritual *and* physical freedom for His image-bearers.

REFLECTION

What aspects of God's love move or shock you the most in the exodus story?

Let My People Love

"And now, Israel, what does the LORD your God require of you,
but to fear the LORD your God, to walk in all his ways, to love him,
to serve the LORD your God with all your heart and with all your soul,
and to keep the commandments and statutes of the LORD,
which I am commanding you today for your good?"

DEUTERONOMY 10:12–13

D id God free the enslaved Hebrews just so they could do whatever they wanted, whenever they wanted, for whichever god they felt like serving that day, if even themselves? That's our modern, counterfeit conception of freedom. God's is much more glorious.

God didn't merely command, "Let my people go!" but, "Let my people go, that they may serve me" (Ex. 10:3). Israel was called out of one slavery into another. But does that sound like freedom? If you understand the two masters at hand, the answer is a resounding *yes.* God freed His people from slavery to a genocidal Pharaoh, who, by the way, likely sported a royal head-dress with the symbol of a snake on it (remember Genesis 3:15?).[77] He freed them to instead serve the One who is, at His very core, love.

God's mission has always been to free humanity from evil's oppressive rule (1 John 3:8). Like Israel, we're never not servants; we're always serving (worshiping) someone or something. Love frees us to rejoice "with the

---

77 Courtney Doctor and Melissa Kruger, *Remember Your Joy: Stories of Salvation* (Austin, TX: The Gospel Coalition, 2022), 77.

truth" (1 Cor. 13:6) that God is the forever-flowing fountain of love, the only Master worth serving. Love liberates us from the abusive relationship we find ourselves in with sin—a degrading, slavish relationship we can't escape on our own.

When love, no matter how thrilling or socially acceptable, is unhinged from the truth of God's Word, it becomes a counterfeit. Indeed, "love is from God" (1 John 4:7), not our personal opinions. Romantic love, familial love, and friendship love—along with all kinds of love, like love of country, nature, or even religion—can all become oppressive when not fully surrendered to Love Himself. Freedom is walking in the truth that God is love, not that your love for (fill in the blank) is god (James 1:25).

Love doesn't say, "Hey, you're free. Do as you please." Love says, "Hey, you're finally free to find your pleasure in Me." God-bought liberty "to love him, to serve the LORD your God" (Deut. 10:12). This is true freedom.

REFLECTION

How have you seen romantic/familial/friendship love, or other kinds of love, become a god in someone's life? What were the effects of this?

What are some ways you sometimes view God's commands as restrictive? What are some of God's rules you find liberating?

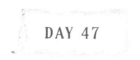
Love's Rescue,
Then Love's Rule

We love because he first loved us.

1 JOHN 4:19

When the fresh-out-of-slavery Israelites crossed through the Red Sea, they were ready for "a land flowing with milk and honey" (Ex. 13:5). What they got first, though, were seven weeks of testing in the desert (Ex. 16–18): hunger, thirst, and war. God was teaching His children about His loving provision and protection. And now, as they reached Mount Sinai, He would teach them, and us, what it means to be in a covenant with Him.

We keep talking about covenants not to sound lofty or archaic, but because covenants are how God organized the plot of Scripture's story. Covenants are relationships, and relationships have rules. For example, would you be okay with your friend gossiping about you? Isn't not to do so, at minimum, an unspoken rule crucial to the relationship's health?

The Hittite covenant format (the suzerain/vassal treaty discussed on Day 20) helps us understand the format of the covenant God made with Israel at Mount Sinai. There's a preamble: Who's in this relationship?; a historical prologue: What has happened between these partners in the past?; the stipulations: rules for the relationship; the public reading: annual rehashing of the relationship; the deposit: where each partner kept his copy of the treaty; and witnesses to the covenant ceremony.[78]

Though this is how God formatted His covenant, Israel's relationship to Him would be something even more profound than that of a vassal/servant to a suzerain/master. If a mere vassal broke the covenant rules, he could expect to be cut out of the covenant (or, quite literally, cut up). But Israel would be a "firstborn son" to their loving Father (Ex. 4:22)—a Father who went great lengths to rescue His child from slavery. And so, God begins His covenant ceremony with a preamble *and* historical prologue: "I am the LORD your God, who brought you out of the land of Egypt, out of the house of slavery" (Ex. 20:2). In other words, before God established the *rules* of the relationship, He reviewed the *who* and the *what already happened* of the relationship.

God's rescue of Israel came *before* God's rules for Israel. To the degree Israel remembered God's merciful redemption, they would be motivated to keep the rules of the relationship. Or, more simply, "We love because he first loved us" (1 John 4:19). And, thankfully, not the other way around.

REFLECTION

We sometimes think, "God will love me if I get really good at obeying." Why is it crucial for us to embrace the correct order of relationship with God ("Because He *already* loves me, I obey")?

---

78 Michael D. Williams, *Far as the Curse Is Found* (Phillipsburg, NJ: P&R Publishing Company, 2005), 140–41.

Love Is the Law

"Hear, O Israel: The LORD our God, the LORD is one.
You shall love the LORD your God with all your heart
and with all your soul and with all your might."

DEUTERONOMY 6:4–5

What's at the very heart of the 613 or so commands given to Israel? We could say it's the Ten Commandments, written by God's own finger, which uphold all the other laws (Ex. 20:3–17; Deut. 5:7–21). We could also say it's all about serving God (Ex. 4:23). But Jesus chose to quote Deuteronomy 6 when He said the greatest command is, "You shall love the Lord your God with all your heart and with all your soul and with all your mind" (Matt. 22:37).

Imagine you're an architect. A potential client says, "Please build my dream home." So you ask him to describe it. He responds, "Just make it beautiful." Confused, you ask him to hand you the basic floor plan he envisions. He responds, "Just make a house I'd love." How could you possibly enter into a contract with this man? The driving force behind the laws God gave Israel can be summed up in one word: love. But if God had simply said, "Just love Me," the Israelites wouldn't have known what that looks like practically.

The fresh-out-of-slavery Hebrews just came out of a land of many gods. So they, like us, needed to learn that loving Yahweh means not serving any other gods (Ex. 20:3). Their contemporaries, the Egyptians and the

Canaanites, worshiped their gods by means of physical objects that represented each deity. So Israel, like us, needed to know that loving Yahweh means not worshiping a carved image of the God who has no physical form or limitations (Ex. 20:4–6). They, like us, needed to know that the God who rescued them takes His name—His character and reputation—seriously enough to prohibit its misuse, acting in any way that misrepresents Him (Ex. 20:7). These ex-slaves needed to know, like us, there is only One who sustains. So they were called to rest on the Sabbath each week (Ex. 20:8–11).

Yahweh had loved His people by rescuing them from the house of slavery. And now He gave them the Mosaic law as a blueprint for how to love Him back: a law of love.

Reflection

What are some implicit rules (rules that go without saying) that come with friendship? What are some explicit rules (rules you need to say aloud) that might come with friendship? How do God's commands help us understand His values, His character, and His concerns?

Jealous:
The Language of Love

Place me like a seal over your heart,
like a seal on your arm;
for love is as strong as death,
its jealousy unyielding as the grave.
It burns like blazing fire,
like a mighty flame.

SONG OF SONGS 8:6 NIV

When the Israelites heard God's law at Mount Sinai, they found out Yahweh is "a jealous God" (Ex. 20:5). In fact, His "name is Jealous" (Ex. 34:14). Could this be love?

God's jealousy is His zeal and passion for His glory to be honored. Divine jealousy is the "flame of the LORD" (Song 8:6), a "consuming fire" (Deut. 4:24; Heb. 12:29) comparable to the intense devotion between spouses that protects their marriage from infidelity. It is holy, pure, and good, "inflamed by the denial of [the worship that] is rightly his."[79]

God's jealousy doesn't contradict His love. God is jealous *because* God is love. If I love my husband, I must be jealous. Indifference in the face of adultery would indicate something deeply wrong with my love as much as

---

79 Jen Wilkin, *Ten Words to Live By: Delighting in and Doing What God Commands* (Wheaton, IL: Crossway, 2021), 34.

his. No wonder it's been said the opposite of love isn't hate but indifference. And God *is* love, so He cannot remain cool when His people embrace lesser lovers, be it the idolizing of sex, comfort, or power. God's jealousy is an expression of His faithful love—a love that won't allow us to fall for counterfeit delights.

God's jealousy should cause us to "rejoice with trembling" (Ps. 2:11). Trembling because we are often an unfaithful bride to our heavenly Husband (Hos. 2:16), loving lesser things—even ourselves—more than Him. Rejoicing because His jealousy doesn't just mean judgment for sinners like us; it means pursuing His adulteress bride with reckless abandon until she's convinced there is no greater lover.

"Love is as strong as death" (Song 8:6)—and the bloodied cross of our Bridegroom proved it.

REFLECTION

The Bible makes a distinction between sinful jealousy (Rom. 13:13; 1 Cor. 3:3; James 3:16) and godly jealousy (Num. 25:1–13; 1 Kings 19:10; 2 Cor. 11:2). What do you think is the difference between the two? Can you think of a time you've experienced one or the other?

Foolish Vine

You blow chills down my spine,
as though a cool breeze
lifted the green leaves
attached to me, this vine,
to expose the underside
intricately designed
inside of me, and I'm
intrigued . . .
So, I suck up
    your water,
        feeling a sense
           of rushing release.
you seem to quench my need
So, I
let my
    roots run deep,
      and
         deeper they go
So, I
grow, this vine,
    reaching out
to you
    around
you,
    all over
you,
    until you
are covered
    with me,
or I
    filled
with you.
    you and I
suddenly
    seem
one.
But, my
    roots stop

when they reach
    a rocky spot
beneath your foundation
my supply of life
running dry, so I
    this vine
tightly *squeeze*
    around you
hoping you'll
    preserve me
because now
my roots are drying,
my green leaves withering, and I
am crying,
"If only I had eyes to see!
This beautiful building,
so elaborately crafted, was
decaying and unstable,
crumbling apart underneath me!"

That cool breeze
    came from the
swinging
    to
and fro
    as my
object of affection
    was
falling,
taking me, this vine,
down
with it
to burn
crushed
underneath
the smoky rubble
of what once
seemed
a strong tower.

And Who Is My Neighbor?

But if anyone has the world's goods and sees his brother in need,
yet closes his heart against him, how does God's love abide in him?

1 JOHN 3:17

Perhaps there's no worse warping of love than corrupt religious reasoning, wriggling its way out of the love's essence. The 600+ laws of the Mosaic covenant—which fleshed out how Israel should love God and people in their social, cultural, and historical location—warn against our knee-jerk, sinful inclinations to excuse ourselves from embodying love.

When an Israelite encountered a poor person, the law warned him: "Take care lest there be an unworthy thought in your heart and you say, 'The seventh year, the year of release is near,' and your eye look grudgingly on your poor brother" (Deut. 15:9). The religious law of the sabbatical year—every seventh year when all debts between Israelites were to be canceled or deferred—was not meant to be an excuse for a lack of generosity in the non-sabbatical years. Religious zeal and biblical knowledge were no cop-out for sacrificial love.

Many religious leaders of Jesus' day were guilty of exactly this (as it is to this day), neglecting "the weightier matters of the law: justice and mercy and faithfulness" (Matt. 23:23). Their lovelessness, disguised behind theological degrees, is often marked by their elaborate intellectual gymnastics, which minimize God's call to sacrificially love the least of society. Books, conferences, and whole seminaries have been dedicated to debunking the necessity of our Spirit-led pursuit of social justice, the very outworking of "love your neighbor as yourself" (Lev. 19:18). All our bending of biblical texts to fit our partisan allegiances, our upper-middle class endeavors, and our lust for power and praise, are summed up in the question of that self-justifying, so-called expert of the biblical law: "And who is my neighbor?" (Luke 10:29).

REFLECTION

> On July 5, 1852, Frederick Douglass delivered an Independence Day speech in New York, titled "The Meaning of July Fourth for the Negro." In answer to his own question, "What, to the American slave, is your 4th of July?" Douglass proclaimed: "I answer: a day that reveals to him, more than all other days in the year, the gross injustice and cruelty to which he is the constant victim."[80] Many professing Christians of Douglass's day used the Bible to justify the demonic slave trade. What are some ways we sometimes close our hearts to compassion for the marginalized today?

---

80 *The Life and Writings of Frederick Douglass*, Volume II, Pre-Civil War Decade 1850–1860, Philip S. Foner (New York, NY: International Publishers Co., Inc. 1950), https://www.pbs.org/wgbh/aia/part4/4h2927t.html.

Love the Vulnerable . . .
As God Does

"You shall not pervert the justice due to the sojourner or to the fatherless,
or take a widow's garment in pledge, but you shall remember that
you were a slave in Egypt and the LORD your God redeemed you from there;
therefore I command you to do this."

DEUTERONOMY 24:17–18

In Lin-Manuel Miranda's musical *In the Heights*, a diverse, immigrant-filled block in Washington Heights, New York, is faced with the threat of gentrification. The main character, Usnavi, runs a bodega (small grocery store) with his cousin Sonny. During a summer blackout, the bodega is threatened by looters. Sonny, who longs for the empowerment of his disenfranchised community, leads a chorus throughout the chaotic scene: "We are powerless, we are powerless!"[81] When God redeemed His enslaved people from Egypt, He wanted them to remember what it felt like to sing that chorus too.

As God prepared His people to live in His place, the Promised Land, with access to His presence—the tabernacle, then eventually the temple—He wanted them to know that in His kingdom those struck by misfortune were by no means at a disadvantage. The land belonged to Yahweh, and it would be allotted to the Israelites as an inheritance (Lev. 20:24; 25:23). But

---

81 Lin-Manuel Miranda, "Blackout," track 12 on *In the Heights—Original Broadway Cast Recording.*

in their patriarchal tribal society, one's access to the land was inextricably linked to one's connection to the oldest living male of the family unit. Can you see why the quartet of the vulnerable—the fatherless, the widow, the immigrant, and the poor—would be at great risk in this society? They were disconnected from a patriarch and/or disconnected from the land, making them susceptible to destitution.

But Yahweh was and is a God who "executes justice for the fatherless and the widow," and "loves the sojourner" (Deut. 10:18–19). And He would do so through His people obeying His law of love, ensuring the holistic well-being of the vulnerable in their society. Read the book of Ruth to see this played out beautifully. Why care for the disadvantaged? "I am the LORD your God, who brought you out of the land of Egypt, out of the house of slavery" (Ex. 20:2; cf. Ex. 22:21–24; Deut. 10:17–19; 24:17–22). Remembering their past collective trauma would help the Israelites liberate those who lived with society's boot on their neck.

Though we may not live in a patriarchal tribal society, God's ethic of sacrificial love for the vulnerable, i.e., justice, extends into the New Testament (Matt. 25:31–46; Luke 4:16–19; James 1:27; 2:14–17).

Love required them to remember they once sang, like Sonny, "We are powerless, we are powerless!" Love required them to ensure no one in their society sang that same song.

REFLECTION

"Religion that is pure and undefiled before God the Father is this: to visit orphans and widows in their affliction, and to keep oneself unstained from the world" (James 1:27). Could it be that "worldliness" includes our apathy toward and villainizing of the oppressed and ill-fortuned among us?

DAY 52

God's Heart: Love Undressed

The LORD passed before him and proclaimed,
"The LORD, the LORD, a God merciful and gracious,
slow to anger, and abounding in steadfast love and faithfulness,
keeping steadfast love for thousands,
forgiving iniquity and transgression and sin,
but who will by no means clear the guilty, visiting the iniquity
of the fathers on the children and the children's children,
to the third and the fourth generation."

EXODUS 34:6–7

While Moses received the law of love at Mount Sinai, the children of Israel were busy crafting a golden calf to worship—a bold breaking of covenant with their covenant-keeping God (Ex. 32; cf. Ex. 24:3). It's in the context of this unspeakable betrayal that God reveals the very core essence of His being—His very heart—to Moses. When God threatens to bring them to the Promised Land without His presence, Moses bravely intercedes for Israel, and even pleads: "Please show me your glory" (Ex. 33:18). In the aftermath of betrayal, God shockingly chooses vulnerability: "I will make all my goodness pass before you and will proclaim before you my name 'the LORD'" (Ex. 33:19). *That* glory, *that* goodness, *that* name is today's passage.

It is this self-revelation of God that holds the story of Scripture together like the spine of a book. It is this undressing, if you will, of God's soul before Moses that all the prophets and poets of Israel cling to for the

151

rest of the Old Testament: "A God merciful and gracious, slow to anger, and abounding in steadfast love and faithfulness" (cf. Ps. 86:15; Joel 2:13; Jonah 4:2). For God to reveal His very soul in this way after being so greatly betrayed by His own people is an act of astonishing, unspeakable love. It's the kind of love the prophet Hosea would be called to model to his unfaithful wife, undressing before her in the most vulnerable act of marital intimacy—again and again—knowing full well her serial adultery (Hos. 1:2). This kind of love is scandalous and, honestly, almost unbelievable.[82]

God's loyal love—His *hesed*—far exceeds our conceptions of loyalty; it's beyond our comprehension (Isa. 55:6–9). Jesus said God's heart is that of a father seeing his rebellious son returning home, feeling a deep compassion for him, and then—in a culturally undignified way—exposing his legs to sprint to him, lavishing him with kisses and his best riches (Luke 15:11–24). The undressing of Love—God's willful exposure of His character, His very heart of love—was Israel's central confession . . . and ours.

The Son of God would expose the depths of this self-revelation Moses heard, when He—publicly undressed and abused—interceded for His murderers, "Father, forgive them, for they know not what they do" (Luke 23:34). His body wasn't the only thing laid bare—so was His heart.

REFLECTION

Why does the context of today's passage matter so much?

---

82 I should note that God calling the prophet Hosea to marry an unfaithful woman was a very specific-to-that-moment-in-history kind of calling to illustrate the nature of Israel's repeated covenant-breaking with Him, and to symbolize for Israel His patience and coming judgment if they wouldn't repent. At no point does Scripture endorse the breaking of marriage vows, nor the need to stay married to an adulterous spouse (Matt. 5:32).

God's Wrath and God's Love

The LORD passed before him and proclaimed,
"The LORD, the LORD, a God merciful and gracious,
slow to anger, and abounding in steadfast love and faithfulness,
keeping steadfast love for thousands,
forgiving iniquity and transgression and sin,
but who will by no means clear the guilty, visiting the iniquity
of the fathers on the children and the children's children,
to the third and the fourth generation."

EXODUS 34:6–7

I've found it impossible to spend only one day on this vital passage about God's very heart—full of faithful love. But how can God be loving *and* wrathful? D. A. Carson explains: "In itself, wrath, unlike love, is not one of the intrinsic perfections of God. Rather, it is a function of God's holiness against sin. Where there is no sin, there is no wrath—but there will always be love in God."[83] How can God love us and have wrath for us at the same time? Dr. Carson continues:

> God has nothing but hate for the sin, but it would be wrong to con-
> clude that God has nothing but hate for the sinner. A difference must
> be maintained between God's view of sin and his view of the sinner. . . .
> God in his perfections must be wrathful against his rebel image-bearers,

---

83 D. A. Carson, *The Difficult Doctrine of the Love of God* (Wheaton, IL: Crossway, 2000), 67.

for they have offended him; God in his perfections must be loving toward his rebel image-bearers, for he is that kind of God.[84]

God's wrath against what's anti-God—namely, evil—is a necessary and glorious expression of His holy character. But the very heart of God (what He delights to show) is *hesed*, even (especially) toward those who know they lack it. Why do you think this is the first thing He declares about Himself? God's merciful, gracious, patient, and steadfast love *is* His glory—it's what gave Moses the boldness to ask for Israel's forgiveness (Ex. 34:8–9). He is "a God ready to forgive" (Neh. 9:17). Like an Olympic sprinter waiting on fingertips and toes for the signal to go, God jumps at the chance to forgive anyone who turns to Him.

Because God is just, He must make right what's been made wrong. But full of *hesed*, He'd prefer things be made right through a person's/people's repentance and His corresponding restoration: "forgiving iniquity and transgression and sin" for the repentant, but "by no means clear[ing] the guilty" after patiently waiting for their repentance, even up "to the third and the fourth generation" of His waiting.

On a bloody Roman cross, God would display His *hesed* by pouring out His wrath for our sin on the sinless One, His own (willing) Son, "that he might be just and the justifier of the one who has faith in Jesus" (Rom. 3:26). What can be said about this kind of love? Everything—and yet nothing that does it justice.

REFLECTION

How do we see both the wrath of God and the love of God meet at the cross of Christ?

---

84 Ibid., 69.

Love's Humble Abode

O LORD, I love the habitation of your house
and the place where your glory dwells.

PSALM 26:8

There's something overpowering about those things that remind us of home—the house you grew up in, the street corner you frequented, the scent of your *abuela's* favorite flower. What makes a place a home? Is it not the people who dwell there?

God rescued His enslaved people to bring them home. Canaan, the Promised Land, was a good land, a fertile land, a land flowing with milk and honey. But the land in itself wasn't home—not if God didn't dwell there.

From the beginning, God has been obsessed with bringing us home to live with Him (Ex. 6:7). It's one of the major themes of Scripture's story. And now, as God proclaimed His law of love from Mount Sinai, He gave instructions on how Israel was to build a tabernacle "that I may dwell in their midst" (Ex. 25:8)—right at the center of the camp. The tabernacle was the throne room of Israel's King, where He "sat" enthroned on the ark of the covenant in an inner room called the holy of holies. Its design was symbolic of Eden, where God first dwelt with His people. Love made a way to dwell with His beloved. He'd always make a way.

As Israel constructed the tabernacle, perhaps they noticed: *Yahweh is choosing to dwell in a tent, like us.* Such condescension to identify with His wilderness-wandering people could only be summed up in a word: love.

The apostle John would one day say of Jesus: "And the Word became flesh and dwelt among us" (John 1:14)—that is, *tabernacled* (tented) among us. Later, the apostle Paul would tell us, "Do you not know that you are God's temple and that God's Spirit dwells in you?" (1 Cor. 3:16). Has love ever had a more humble abode?

REFLECTION

When have you most felt at home? What made you feel that way? In what ways might you view your own story as a search for home?

"Where are you?"

I'm in the cool breeze
underneath the pavilion's shade
on a typical summer day.
I'm underneath the sound
of birds singing
kids swimming, playing
and the general chit-chatting
of Wirz Park in Casselberry.
I'm in Mamita's neighborhood
eyes drained of water
from standing on what's always been
sacred ground: 48 Winding Ridge Road
    my home
    my safe space
    the place life slowed down
    to a sweet pace
    where the world was right-
       side-up again
where I wish I could come in to that
    little house
    my cheek kissed
    my nose met
    with the smell of café
    my ears
    the clattering of dishes
where I wish I could hug her again
sit on her orchid-filled porch
talk about anything and everything
'til I slowly leave
with many false starts
toward the front door.

I'm at her neighborhood park

where Gab and I would race
I'm staring at the basketball court
where I once played pick-up with Tito Gary
(the court felt much bigger then)
Those aged trees, dancing now in the
    breeze,
they probably remember me
seems they wave even now to me.
we share roots, you know.
I grin with salt-encrusted cheeks
and nod back at them.
somehow, I know they understand.

I'm in the place of a million memories
almost all of them perfectly sweet
almost all of them so secretly sacred
their divine nature
once so unbeknownst to me.
Now, I think I see.
I watch younger me running
around here: free.
I feel her sitting next to me,
sweating, hair messy,
allowing herself to dream.
I'm with the very best of my past
soaked in sweet, deep sadness
nostalgia's embrace
but in the best way—my grief
being honored
while I take in deep breaths
of summer breeze
wondering if it's the same
that once brushed across

my sun-kissed kid face,
made its way around the world
to find me back here again.
It's gotta be the same breeze.
I can hear Mamita's laugh in it.

For me, this is sacred land
     where my family's story (Mom's
       side)
re-began.
where mine has, too.

It's a pretty neglected, underdeveloped
  town
and it's where my heart is most
     where my feet first grew roots.
The sign at the park says "Casselberry,
  The Garden District"
and that sounds about right to me.
it's the place
of my story's pleasantness,
my "Garden of Eden."

I'm drawn here by something
guttural, deep, a longing
I can't ignore for too long
for a song of my story
for your promise of renewing
to sing over me, restoring the years
those dead ends, those locusts
those scary things of scarcity
have stolen.

Here, Lord.
I'm here.
Holy ground because
You're here with me.

I'm weeping. I'm silent.
I'm listening.

DAY 55

Access to Love

I will come into your house with burnt offerings;
I will perform my vows to you . . .
I will offer to you burnt offerings of fattened animals,
with the smoke of the sacrifice of rams;
I will make an offering of bulls and goats.

PSALM 66:13–15

Love brings others in. But sin, by nature, doesn't like to live with God's holiness. So God graciously provided a way for His people to have access to Him, even after they had sinned: the sacrificial system. The law of love wasn't only about setting a holy standard for God's people. It provided a pathway back to a right relationship with God when, not if, they strayed.

We saw a glimpse of it when God clothed Adam and Eve with the skins of an animal (Gen. 3:21). But now God would institute a sacrificial system that allowed for atonement—*at-one-ment*, reconciliation with God. The burnt, grain, peace, sin, and guilt offerings allowed God's people to have fellowship with Him: offering praise, petitions, and confessions with the blood of unblemished animals like bulls and goats. Because of the sacrificial system, all of God's people could proclaim: "Blessed be God, because he has not rejected my prayer or removed his steadfast love from me!" (Ps. 66:20). But their prayers were accepted because another was rejected—innocent animals were condemned in their place.

Could *all* the blood of *all* the bulls and goats on *all* the earth ever fully cover *all* our countless sins? No. "It is impossible for the blood of bulls and goats to take away sins" (Heb. 10:4). But through the constant blood flow in the tabernacle—and later, the temple—God's people saw a shadow of the "once for all" (Heb. 10:10) sacrifice God would provide through His Son. A sacrifice that would grant us "confidence to enter the holy places by the blood of Jesus . . . through his flesh" (Heb. 10:19–20). A sacrifice that would give us eternal access to God's love, even after we've sinned again and again.

REFLECTION

How do you view God's love when you sin, especially when you commit the same sin you just recently confessed? How might remembering Christ's "once for all" sacrifice encourage you to come back to God with confidence that He "has not removed his steadfast love" from you? For further meditation, read Luke 5:1–11 and notice how Jesus responds to Peter's fearful admission that he was a sinner.

An Omnipotent Love

"And now, please let the power of the Lord be great as you have promised,
saying, 'The LORD is slow to anger and abounding in steadfast love,
forgiving iniquity and transgression, but he will by no means clear the guilty,
visiting the iniquity of the fathers on the children, to the third and
the fourth generation.' Please pardon the iniquity of this people,
according to the greatness of your steadfast love,
just as you have forgiven this people, from Egypt until now."

NUMBERS 14:17–19

From the very beginning of their journey to the Promised Land, Israel suffered from severe spiritual amnesia: they kept forgetting God's love and power that had rescued them from slavery. So they grumbled against God and against Moses, and they fantasized going back to slavery in Egypt— even calling the place of their enslavement "a land flowing with milk and honey" (Num. 16:13). Wild. Isn't that the temptation we face when unfulfilled longings and unanswered prayers threaten our faith in God's love?

This may be wrong, but I deserve a little pleasure. I've suffered enough . . .
I'm done caring for others. No one has cared for me—not even God . . .
God isn't interested in my life. He's too busy blessing everyone else . . .
What's the point of praying when nothing is changing?

About halfway to the Promised Land, Israel rebelled again: "Why is the LORD bringing us into this land, to fall by the sword? . . . Let us choose a leader and go back to Egypt" (Num. 14:3–4). The very generation who felt the sting of the whip longed to return to it. In the wilderness, they put the Lord to the test "these ten times" (Num. 14:22) just like Pharaoh. As it's been said: they may have been out of Egypt, but Egypt was not out of them.

As Moses interceded, yet again, for them, notice what he banked on: "The LORD is slow to anger and abounding in steadfast love." The very heart of God once revealed to him (Ex. 34:5–7). God is, at His core, bubbling over with steadfast love. And what does it take for God to "pardon the iniquity of this people"? It takes "the power of the Lord." The force of God's omnipotence is channeled toward mercy for His people. God's love is not a fluctuating, weak-kneed sentimentalism. His love is resolute and reliable—stronger than sin itself.

A just judgment on the exodus generation proceeded, but God would keep His promise to Abraham. His descendants would dwell in the Promised Land. God would exercise His power, not just to judge His rebellious people but, more surprisingly, to show His steadfast love.

REFLECTION

God chooses to channel His omnipotence toward showing you kindness each day. How does this affect the way you think about power and strength (God's and your own)?

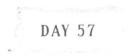

A Protective Love

But the LORD your God would not listen to Balaam;
instead the LORD your God turned the curse into a blessing for you,
because the LORD your God loved you.

DEUTERONOMY 23:5

As Israel wandered for forty years in the wilderness, they faced multiple wars with nations who were intimidated by Israel's testimony.

Balak, the prince of Moab, was no exception. But instead of approaching Israel with swords and arrows, Balak thought it best to hire Balaam, the best sorcerer he knew, to "curse this people for me, since they are too mighty for me" (Num. 22:6). Balaam, despite his disingenuous proclamations of faith in Yahweh, obliged. Three times. And yet, three times the Spirit of God filled his mouth: "How can I curse whom God has not cursed?" (Num. 23:8). Instead of cursing God's people, Balaam could only bless them. Echoes of God's promise to Abraham rang through Balaam's prophecies: "I will bless those who bless you, and him who dishonors you I will curse" (Gen. 12:3).

But notice what Israel was up to while God was protecting them: grumbling (Num. 16:11, 41), quarreling (Num. 20:3), and speaking against God (Num. 21:5). Like a mother removing a shard of glass from a toddler's path, God was protecting Israel when they didn't even know it. God's love is unbreakable. It's a shield against the loudest libels, the craziest curses, and the worst wishes anyone could ever hurl your way.

God's love is even more sure than the condemnation you hurl at yourself. "Who shall bring any charge against God's elect? It is God who justifies. Who is to condemn? Christ Jesus is the one who died—more than that, who was raised—who is at the right hand of God, who indeed is interceding for us" (Rom. 8:33–34). When God determines to bless, none can curse—at least not successfully. When God determines to love, none can object—at least not successfully.

REFLECTION

Your story is filled with much more than you could ever perceive. Can you imagine all God has protected you from today? This month? This year? Take some time to thank Him for His loving protection, which expands beyond your awareness.

A Loving Author,
A Progressing Plot

And the LORD your God will circumcise your heart
and the heart of your offspring, so that you will love the LORD your God
with all your heart and with all your soul, that you may live.

DEUTERONOMY 30:6

Moses was about to die. His forty-year wilderness journey came to a close as "the Lord showed him all the land" (Deut. 34:1) he wouldn't step foot on because of his own sin. What must he have felt? There had never been a rescue greater than the exodus (Deut. 4:34). There had never been a law so holy as God's for Israel (Deut. 4:8). And yet, the very people who saw the Red Sea split rejected the God who accomplished it.

The story of Israel is a microcosm of humanity's story. We, too, rebel against basic moral standards despite God's day-to-day kindness toward us (Rom. 2:14–15). We, too, grow discontent with daily bread. We, too, are in need of a circumcised heart—a fundamental revolution of our innermost being that is resistant to loving God. The story of Israel is also a repetition of Adam and Eve's story. The same God who abundantly provided every tree of the garden was the same God who rained manna from heaven. And He was the same God accused of being loveless (Gen. 3:1; Deut. 1:27). In fact, the rest of the Old Testament is somewhat cyclical: God displays His love, His people reject His love, God brings judgment, some of His people repent, God lovingly restores. Rinse and repeat.

I'm sure I don't have to tell you that your life, and mine, can be rather cyclical as well. We are shaped by our childhood relationships and experiences, and though we may grow out of some of those environments and patterns, our life's story is replete with repetitive mistakes, reenacted trauma, and unremitting questions at the core of our souls:

Am I utterly broken?
Am I utterly alone?
Am I an utter failure?
Am I utterly unlovable?

Your story, like mine, is a journey in which you find yourself asking, much more than once, *How did I get here again? Why am I still struggling with this?* And yet, like Scripture, the cyclical nature of your story does not mean its plot isn't progressing. The sun repeats the same course every day, but that doesn't mean time stands still. Ancient Israel repeated its rebellions throughout its history, but that doesn't mean God wasn't moving toward "the fullness of time" (Gal. 4:4).

This need for a new heart echoes throughout the Old Testament as leader after leader fell short of the law of love. The power it takes for a holy God to love sinners is the same power sinners need to love a holy God. And one day, God would grant that power. Redemptive history was moving toward glory, despite the cycles. So is your story.

Reflection

Think about the nature of your relationships: with God, family, friends, coworkers, romantic partners, and so on. What are some conflicts and wounds you've seen repeated in those relationships? What difference does it make to know that the loving Author of your life is dedicated to progressing the plot of your story toward glory despite its discouraging cycles?

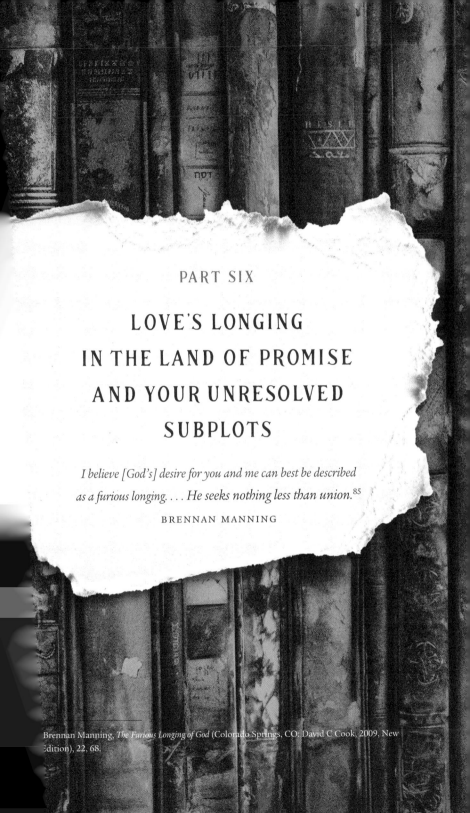

PART SIX

LOVE'S LONGING IN THE LAND OF PROMISE AND YOUR UNRESOLVED SUBPLOTS

*I believe [God's] desire for you and me can best be described
as a furious longing. . . . He seeks nothing less than union.*[85]

BRENNAN MANNING

Brennan Manning, *The Furious Longing of God* (Colorado Springs, CO: David C Cook, 2009, New
Edition), 22, 68.

The prosperity of promised land
might prove more perilous
than thirst and tents
of wilderness weaknesses.

— *getting settled vs. settling*

Settling, Would They Settle?

The sorrows of those who run after another god shall multiply.

PSALM 16:4

Be very careful, therefore, to love the LORD your God.

JOSHUA 23:11

Finally! The second tidal wave of God's great redemption story begins! After forty years of wilderness wandering, the children of Israel (the generation after those of the exodus that rebelled), were ready for that Eden-like land of "milk and honey" (Josh. 5:6)—Canaan. God was ready to plant them in the land He promised Abraham (Gen. 15:18–20). He brought them *out* (of slavery) to bring them *in* (to settlement). Led by Moses' successor, Joshua, they could finally pursue God's promised rest in the land they longed for all these years. But the promise didn't nullify their need to obey (Josh. 1:13; cf. Heb. 4:8–11).

To enter into that rest, they had to obey the command to conquer Canaan—a unique-to-that-exact-moment-in-history call to execute God's justice on the outrageous corruption of the Canaanites. As Adam was supposed to drive out any evil encroachments in Eden, so Israel needed to do so in this "new Eden" (if you will), lest they become ensnared in the same evil.[86]

---

86 This was not genocide but a cleansing of the land from oppressive religious/cultural norms that defiled it and would defile God's people. Note the Canaanites' sexual abuses in Leviticus 18; their child abuse and murder in Deuteronomy 12:29–31. Further, not all Canaanites were killed (Deut. 7:22; cf. Ex. 23:30; Judg. 2:1–5; 3:1–5), and Yahweh's law was that Israel pursue peace with all the other nations (Deut. 20:10). The story of Joshua is about God (partially) fulfilling His promises to Abraham in that generation.

As Noah's ark-building became a warning sign to his corrupt generation, so Yahweh's victorious track record from the exodus to His people's Promised-Land entrance provided generations of Canaanites the opportunity to turn to the One who patiently waits for repentance—*even up to four generations* (Ex. 34:6–8; cf. Ex. 20:5; Deut. 9:5)! In fact, some from Egypt did join God's people at the exodus (Ex. 12:38), and now at Jericho the prostitute Rahab did the same (Josh. 2)—a shining example of Yahweh's heart to expand His covenant family (Matt. 1:5). But most of the Canaanites rejected Yahweh, just as He said would happen "in the fourth generation" (Gen. 15:16). Once again, judgment and salvation were coupled.

Bright beginnings and (partially) fulfilled promises came in Joshua's day. But witnessing God's promises kept required a heart check. Joshua brought before them the same covenant question God placed before humanity in Eden: as God settled them in the land, would they settle for lesser loves?

REFLECTION

When God grants you a victory of any type, what are some temptations you face? Look up Psalms 62:10; 106:34–39; Proverbs 30:7–9; 1 Kings 11:1–8; Matthew 18:21–35; Luke 10:17–20; 17:11–19.

Though "the earth is the LORD's and the fullness thereof" (Ps. 24:1), God graciously gave Canaan to Abraham's descendants at this point in redemptive history. Why? "Giving a land as part of the project of redemption highlights that God is committed to his created order and to the redemption of human society."[87] For further contemplation on the relationship between Israel, Christians, and the Promised Land, might I recommend the essay "Ecclesiology and the Theology of the Land: A Palestinian Christian Perspective" by Munther Isaac?[88]

---

87 Munther Isaac, "Ecclesiology and the Theology of the Land: A Palestinian Christian Perspective," in *Majority World Theology: Christian Doctrine in Global Context*, ed. Gene L. Green et al. (Westmont, IL: InterVarsity Press, 2020), 578.
88 Ibid., 577–89.

Love's Light in the Dark Ages

"He shall be to you a restorer of life and a nourisher of your old age,
for your daughter-in-law who loves you,
who is more to you than seven sons, has given birth to him."

RUTH 4:15

The Israelites' obedience to God's law of love was meant to be a light in this dark world, enlightening other nations about the God who saves (Deut. 4:1–8).[89] But after that first Promised Land–generation, Israel settled for lesser loves, chasing after "the gods of the peoples who were around them" (Judg. 2:12). They descended into a two-hundred-year, cyclical dark age: their idolatry, Yahweh's judgment, their cry for help, Yahweh's rescue through a judge (warrior), then back to their idolatry. Rinse and repeat.[90] When God's people don't live like God's people, who suffers the most? Society's vulnerable: the poor, widow, fatherless, and foreigner. But a beam of hope broke through the dark ages—shining from the extreme margins of society.

Ruth, Naomi, and Boaz formed what I like to call a "triangle of *hesed*" with Yahweh in the center of it. God doesn't directly speak in the book of Ruth, yet His commitment to covenant kindness (*hesed*) is loud and

---

89 Cf. Isaiah 42:6; Matthew 5:14–15; Philippians 2:14–16.
90 The now-settled Israelites assumed Yahweh was an as-needed god of military and historical events, and the gods of fertility (the Baals) were the day-to-day gods for healthy crops and children. So they'd cry out to Yahweh when bullied by neighboring nations, then go back to the Baals once the dust settled.

clear—mediated by His covenant people applying His Word in their lives. Ruth, a widowed foreigner (Moabite), left the security and gods of her nation to serve her bereaved mother-in-law Naomi, and to cling to Yahweh (Ruth 1). Boaz, a wealthy Israelite and relative of Naomi, followed the heart of Yahweh's laws to care for foreigners, abundantly providing for Ruth in his fields (Ruth 2). Naomi, bereaved and bitter at first, grew in hope enough to strategize a plan to prevent Ruth's destitution (Ruth 3). Ruth, in a shocking plot twist, then proposed to Boaz that they apply Yahweh's laws of redemption (of land and lineage: Lev. 25; Deut. 25) through marriage in order to benefit not just Ruth, but Naomi—providing for Naomi an heir (Ruth 3–4). Boaz, knowing the scope of this financial sacrifice, agreed to Ruth's plan, and they gave birth to Naomi's redeemer: Obed, "the father of Jesse, the father of David" (Ruth 4:17).

The interplay of sacrificial love between these three is guided by the (Mosaic) law of love. And God uses this triangle of *hesed* to move His people from the dark ages of the judges to a king "after [God's] own heart" (1 Sam. 13:14). Cycles of sin couldn't stop God's redemptive plot from progressing, and He'd continue to use the unlikely, like Ruth, to progress His plan.

God gave Ruth agency to sacrificially love, making her a sort of coauthor in Scripture's love story—partnering with God, as in Eden, to display His glorious love to the ends of the earth. But could she have ever imagined being written into King David's lineage—much less the lineage of our ultimate Redeemer (Matt. 1:5; Gal. 4:4–6)?

REFLECTION

Can you imagine the ripple effect of redemption God will bring to this world, even generations from now, because you choose to love Him by sacrificially loving others today?

Hannah, Silent Sister[91]

The LORD had closed her womb
He closed her womb
He did not keep Hannah from
unfulfilled desire, distress and hurt
He closed her womb. He ordained
    her pain
on her way to worship
on her way to worship
Every year, the same:
longing, no child
watching, no mercy from her rival
How could she eat? She wept bitterly.

> How can You *withhold*
> from me
> my good desire
> my good desire . . .

Her husband loved her
couldn't understand
wasn't he enough?
wasn't he enough?
worth more than ten sons?

> *All your food and wine*
> *won't fulfill me.*

She arose
   Come.
She arose

> *I have no portion in this life*
> *apart from You*
> *I have no need to hide*
> my deep distress.

I come.

She vowed a vow and said,
Look on my affliction
LORD of hosts
Remember me,
I am Your servant
Don't forget me
I am Your servant
If You'd grant me a son
for I am Your servant
I will give Him to You
he will be Your servant.

> *Take, take*
> *this desire that runs strong*
> *in my veins*
> *this desire that hurts*
> *good desire, unfulfilled*
> *this pain.*
> *Take, take*
> *my longing, and give it*
> *if You will*
> *and I will give it back*
> *in worship*
> *for my desire is Yours*
> *this, too, is for You.*

She wouldn't leave her King's presence
Oh, Hannah, silent sister
Eli thought he saw you
but you saw only your God
you saw only your God

---

91 1 Samuel 1:1–2:11.

My heart speaks, but no sound
comes from my mouth
My lips move, but no sound
comes from my mouth
My tears will worship
You will interpret groans.

Eli took her as drunk
but she honestly confessed
her condition was much
more overwhelming:
My spirit is distressed!

I will honestly say
where I am today
Why should a plastic mask conceal
my troubled soul
my troubled soul?

I have been pouring out my soul
before the LORD
So here I am,
with great anxiety
and vexation
pouring out my soul
before the LORD.

Oh, Hannah, silent sister
broken, open
pouring out your soul
Go in peace
May the God of Israel grant what
   you seek
May the God of Israel grant what
   you seek.

I am also your servant, servant of
   God,

May I find favor in your eyes, favor
though man consider me despised

I will arise
when you strengthen me
to stand and eat
for Your joy fulfills me
You are my portion
with nothing yet from Your hand
I will rejoice, I will arise
and worship
Early, I will worship
before You.

She returned
and her husband knew her
God remembered her
Elkanah loved her
God did not forget her.

I ordained
that you would be grieved
that you would want a good thing
want a good thing
And I would
more increasingly be
your everything
your every good thing
And I would be
your portion, your very good thing
And you would run to me, your joy
your fulfillment—not deceived
to believe your hope
was in a gift, for your hope
is in Me.
I ordained
that you would worshipfully mourn
and petition and see

I hear your prayers
and I am moved
in My sovereignty
I am moved
and I remember you
my servant, my servant
I am your good thing.

She kept her vow
and her faith was proved genuine
she nursed her child
and gave him back to the LORD:
He is the greatest good, my joy
and my son, my Samuel,
will be His servant.
I have been heard by God
and I am satisfied.

> *I am known by God*
> *and I am satisfied.*

Samuel, so young
he was the LORD's
Hannah's gift had come
and he was the LORD's.

No silence this time
she came
with a bull, flour, wine
her Samuel she gave
and the temple was filled with
loud praise
Eli worshiped
Hannah prayed.

> *I must not*
> *withhold this thanks.*
> *I can't!*
> *For what you've given me*

has shown me
who You are.
You've fulfilled me!
I overflow with joy,
not just in the gift,
but in Your salvation
yes, Your holiness
perfect wisdom, omniscience
Your compassion
how You care for the lowly
Sovereign King, You know me
Oh, You know me!
I exalt in Your strength
I worship You only!

The LORD had closed her womb
silenced her voice, opened her heart
and her hand.
He was her portion.

Oh, Hannah, silent sister
how you were heard
and remembered by your Lord.

Despite Deluded Demands, Love Reigns

Put not your trust in princes. . . .
The LORD will reign forever.

PSALM 146:3, 10

During the dark ages of the judges—with a few exceptions, like Deborah, Jael, and Ruth—exclusive faithfulness to Yahweh was elusive. But God, true to His merciful habit of magnifying the marginalized, worked through a bullied, barren Hannah to birth the greatest judge of Israel, Samuel—a prophet who listened to the voice of God amidst the moral failures of Israel's spiritual leaders (1 Sam. 1–7). Samuel would anoint and mentor the most important king of Israel, David, Ruth's great-grandson. But before this, Israel demanded a king "like all the nations" (1 Sam. 8:5)—opposing God's intention to choose, in His timing, the kind of king He'd want to shepherd His people (Deut. 17:14–20).

God's people were supposed to differ from the rest of the world to display that Eden-like blessing of life under God's loving reign (Deut. 28:1–14). But under the ongoing threat of the technologically advanced, displaced, and desperate Philistines, Israel demanded and received in King Saul the kind of king God warned them about: one who would take and not give, who would seek to be served and not serve (1 Sam. 8:10–18; cf. Mark 10:42–45). Though God knew "they have rejected me from being king over them"

(1 Sam. 8:7), He graciously used Israel's deluded demand, fueled by their desire to *be like* the rest of the world and yet to *be protected from* the rest of the world, to distinctly develop three crucial covenant offices in the Promised Land: prophet, priest, and king.

These offices were already mapped out in the Mosaic law: the priests would represent the people to God, offering sacrifices on their behalf (Ex. 40:12–15); the king would be the covenant representative for Israel *without* absolute power because he'd govern under Yahweh's guidance in the Mosaic law, acknowledging God as the true King of Israel (Deut. 17:14–20); and the prophet would speak God's words to God's people and the king, beckoning the king and the people to return to the law of love when they strayed (Deut. 13:1–5).

You could think of these offices like characters in a play that are developed through the overarching story of the production. These crucial roles would be played out through the drama of Israel's history in preparation for the ultimate Prophet, Priest, and King, who would perfectly exemplify *hesed* (faithful love) on both God *and* Israel's side of the covenant relationship (Rev. 22:16). God's plan of cosmic-spreading love would prevail—not just *despite* Israel's doubt-driven demand, but even *through* it.

Reflection

Waiting on the Lord to move in an area of genuine need can be a painful endeavor (ask Hannah). Our stories are filled with our pursuit of earthly substitutes instead of faith in God's loving provision, protection, and pleasure (ask those Israelites). What might it look like for you to lay your longings before Love (like Hannah), dethroning the lowercase "kings" in your heart (unlike Israel)—making more room for His reigning love?

A Forever-House
Founded on Forever-Love

My steadfast love I will keep for him forever, and my covenant
will stand firm for him. I will establish his offspring forever
and his throne as the days of the heavens.

PSALM 89:28–29

After King Saul forfeited his family's chance at a dynasty because of his faithlessness, God gave David the throne. David was the shepherd-turned-king who God wanted to appoint for Israel (Deut. 17:14–20)—one who delighted in God's law of love (1 Sam. 13:14), owned up to his own corruption and its consequences (2 Sam. 12; Ps. 51), and "administered justice and equity to all his people" (2 Sam. 8:15). Through King David, God unified the tribes of Israel into one nation, giving His people "rest" from the threat of surrounding nations (2 Sam. 7:1)—bringing Israel closer to the fulfillment of the land promise God made to Abraham (Gen. 15:18–20).

God had settled King David in his house in Jerusalem, so David thought, *Why not build a house (temple) for God's special presence to settle, instead of the temporal tent of the tabernacle?* But God, with wonderful wordplay, declared, "the LORD will make you a house" (2 Sam. 7:11)—that is, a dynasty (house) of kings directly descending from David that would lead God's people until a king, *the* King, from David's lineage would reign "forever" (2 Sam. 7:13). Israel's kings were called the "anointed ones"—*messiahs*—anointed with oil to represent the power of the Holy Spirit setting them apart for a specific service.[92] Through David would come *the* Anointed One (*the* Messiah).

Until then, God would continue David's dynasty (house) of kings, promising "my steadfast love will not depart from him" (2 Sam. 7:15), even though God would discipline these kings when they strayed from the law of love. This special promise to David is known as the Davidic covenant. God masterfully wove the kingship role into His drama of redemption by using the Davidic dynasty—the house of David, founded on God's forever-love—to set the stage for the drama's main character: the final and forever King of Israel.

Many generations later, the angel Gabriel would announce to Mary, the mother of Jesus: "the Lord God will give to him the throne of his father David . . . and of his kingdom there will be no end" (Luke 1:32–33). But this Messiah-King—translated as *Christ* in the Greek of the New Testament—would bring a kingdom most didn't expect. He'd serve the suffering and move mightily among the marginalized. A house-less King (Matt. 8:20), He'd make us the "living stones" of His "spiritual house" (1 Peter 2:5). In this Messiah, we inherit that promise of God's enduring love given to King David, becoming a kingdom *under* His dominion, to reign *with* Him "forever and ever" (Rev. 22:5).

What do you do when the historical weight of God's promise of "forever and ever" love falls on your soul like a waterfall? Only one thing makes sense. You bow down under the weight of His worthiness, and, like David, you worship: "Therefore you are great, O Lord God. For there is none like you" (2 Sam. 7:22). Not even close.

REFLECTION

Why is worship the proper response to God's love for you? Also see Romans 12:1.

---

92 Hannah alluded to God's "anointed one" in her song-prayer (1 Sam. 2:10; cf. 1 Sam. 16:13).

Lineages of Lasting Love

"I, Jesus, . . . am the root and the descendant of David,
the bright and morning star."

REVELATION 22:16

Raise your hand if you've ever felt your brain begin to doze a bit when you get to the sections of Scripture that go something like this: so-and-so fathered so-and-so, who fathered so-and-so, and so on? (My hand is raised.) What do these seemingly boring genealogies have to do with the grand drama of love God was and is writing and directing?

You could think of Scripture's long lists of genealogies like the narrator's voice at a play, booming from somewhere behind the curtain, helping us connect the various subplots, or side stories, and characters of the drama so we can better understand the main plot's point. The genealogies help us find our historical footing when the story of Scripture unfolds into its kaleidoscope variety of stories. They help us see that the ancient promises of God, from Eve to Mary, are trustworthy and true—"from generation to generation" (Luke 1:50). God's love is faithful: when He makes a promise, He keeps it. And the genealogies help us see that.

Remember the main point of Scripture's drama? God is redeeming a people for Himself through His Son to renew (resurrect) the entire universe in perfect unity and harmony under His loving kingship. It's the greatest story ever told, and also the longest story ever told. That promised Seed of Eve, who would crush the serpent's head (Gen. 3:15), rendering evil inept, would be:

the descendant of David, given a promise (2 Sam. 7:12–16), who was

the descendant of Judah, given a promise (Gen. 49:10), who was

the descendant of Abraham, given a promise (Gen. 17:4–7), who was

the descendant of Noah, given a promise (Gen. 9:8–11), who was

the descendant of Seth (Gen. 4:26), who was

the descendant of Adam.

The New Testament begins with a genealogy that, instead of putting us to sleep, should, if we've been paying attention, make us jump out of our seats: "The book of the genealogy of Jesus Christ, the son of David, the son of Abraham" (Matt. 1:1). There, at center stage, we find that the narrator behind the curtain is not only the writer, director, and producer of this drama—but the very star of the show. The whole play hangs on Him!

God's special covenant with David (2 Sam. 7) looked forward *and* it looked back. It expanded and further clarified the covenant God established with Abraham, and it looked forward to the coming of the Davidic King who would reign forever. So, when we pray, as David did, "The LORD will fulfill his purpose for me; Your steadfast love, O LORD, endures forever. Do not forsake the work of your hands" (Ps. 138:8), we *look back* at these genealogies as lineages of God's lasting love, so we can *look forward* with fortified faith that our stories—past, present, and future—are safe in the Great Playwright's hands. The whole drama still hangs on Him.

REFLECTION

Why is looking back at God's past promises fulfilled crucial for us to be able to look forward with hope?

Has Anyone Been a Truer Friend?

Friends come and friends go, but a true friend sticks by you like family.

PROVERBS 18:24 MSG[93]

We can't talk about Scripture's love story without reflecting on one of its greatest friendships. My father-in-law has said that in the end, you're blessed if you have one, maybe even two, friendships that truly stand the test of time. Having experienced a stinging string of lost friendships— from death, distance, and devastating fallouts—I've found this reality check rather humbling. Maybe you can relate. But in Jonathan and David's friendship we find conviction, comfort, and an incredible archetype of the great love story of Scripture—a story about the lengths God went to make us His friends.

Jonathan and David's friendship was shocking, considering Jonathan's father was the jealous-turned-murderous King Saul who kept David on the run for years. In the midst of his father's spiritual and mental decline, Jonathan—who would've been heir to the throne—amazingly accepted David as the true "anointed one" Yahweh chose. He even made a covenant with David, promising to protect David from his own father, while David promised to protect Jonathan's descendants (1 Sam. 20). *Hesed* recognized *hesed*. Jonathan saw in David the same love for God he had, and so "he loved him as his own soul" (1 Sam. 18:3). Faith in God's steadfast love (*hesed*) was the basis of their friendship.

---

93 Scripture quotation marked MSG are taken from The Message, copyright © 1993, 2002, 2018 by Eugene H. Peterson. Used by permission of NavPress. All rights reserved. Represented by Tyndale House Publishers.

After Jonathan tragically died in battle, along with King Saul, David cried, "your love to me was extraordinary, surpassing the love of women" (2 Sam. 1:26). Many of us can't imagine friendship-love running deeper than romantic-love. But David could—enough to fulfill his part of the covenant, even when his friend had passed. Truly, "a friend loves at all times" (Prov. 17:17).

The typical move in David's day would've been to kill everyone from the previous regime's family once he became king, removing any threat of insurrection. But David went out of his way to find Jonathan's son, Mephibosheth, to "show him kindness [*hesed*] for Jonathan's sake" (2 Sam. 9:1). Mephibosheth was the grandson of the man who consistently attempted murder on David. But, to his utter shock, death was not on the menu. David came to restore Saul's land to him and invited him to eat "at the king's table" (2 Sam. 9:13) forever, "like one of the king's sons" (2 Sam. 9:11). Mephibosheth, disabled from an early childhood injury, received the blessings of a friendship that ran deeper than familial bonds—one that stood the test of time.

Our Creator-King invited us into His friendship. Though we rejected it, He sought us out, making covenant promises to Noah, Abraham, and David of a forever-love that unfolded for generations until His Son poured wine—"the new covenant in my blood" (Luke 22:20)—and told His friends, "I will not drink again of this fruit of the vine until that day when I drink it new *with you* in my Father's kingdom" (Matt. 26:29; emphasis mine). That same night, the Messiah-King said, "No one has greater love than this: to lay down his life for his friends" (John 15:13 CSB). And then, with a love surpassing any romance, He did. All this so we, too, could feast at His table in the banquet of His love (Matt. 8:11)—not merely His servants, but as He calls us: His friends (John 15:15).

REFLECTION

Message a friend today to tell him or her what ways they've shown you the love of Jesus. Get specific.

The Best of Men

the best of men
wipe your tears
sit in silence as you grieve.
yet
the best of men
still go to sleep
and you are left to step
alone
into that
dark garden of death
you cry out on your own.

in the end, aren't we all alone?

while the best of men
wear finite skin
the Son of Man
sits, leans in
stays with you
in the dark garden
he was once there too, for you
alone, so you
would never be
without
The Best of men
again.

How Did We Get Here?

Look, O LORD, for I am in distress;

my stomach churns;

my heart is wrung within me,

because I have been very rebellious.

LAMENTATIONS 1:20

Not all stories are best told with a plot that flows from beginning, to middle, to end. And not all histories are best voiced by the victor. Most of Scripture's story is declared from society's margins, through the mouths of the oppressed, destitute, and seemingly forgotten.

So, imagine with me: you're from the tribe of Judah. As a kid, you knew God promised your tribe "a scepter" that would never "depart"—an heir to David who'd reign forever (Gen. 49:10; 2 Sam. 7). You're Abraham's descendant—promised the land you live in (Gen. 15; 2 Chron. 6:6). You're Yahweh's "treasured possession among all peoples" (Ex. 19:5). This is your people's story, their identity; it's *your* story, *your* identity.

And yet, it's 581 BC—about five years after the great fall of your home-town, Jerusalem, at the hands of the cruel, mighty nation Babylon. At age twelve, your coming of age came with the cries of mothers bereaved, fathers deported, blood pouring in the decimated streets by men speaking some language you couldn't understand. Prophets like Isaiah and Jeremiah warned of this exile, this destruction of the temple, this Davidic dynasty destroyed—but they'd been mostly ignored, scorned, persecuted. Sure, the Assyrian exile had happened to the seceded northern nation of Israel (chronic idolaters), but here in Judah? The place of promise? Now, only

185

"the poorest in the land" (Jer. 40:7) are left. And that's you. This is your story, but your identity?

When you walk by the Babylonian soldiers occupying your lonely city, your parents' eyes tell the story their mouths can't articulate: deportation is vile. You've seen girls violated, boys enslaved, starved mothers eating their own babies. Law enforcement calls you names, dehumanizing and demoralizing. You want to hide. You want to fight. You want to scream. *How?! God, why?!*

As my culture collapses, my family's future all but dead—
where is Yahweh in all of this?
Were all those promises just fairy tales, mere myths?
Is Yahweh just like the gods of our neighbors—temperamental, vindictive?
Did the Babylonian gods defeat Him?
If He's really the One writing history, and our history with Him, then
how could God be good when all I see is chaos and destruction?

Your questions are valid. Read that again. Now take that rage, that sadness, that pain, and send it all to heaven's address. Make it a song of worship, a prayer to God. This is called lament. This is not only okay to do; lament is crucial to your learning—deep in your bones—the love of God, which will meet you, hold you, and surprise you on the mourning path. Yes, even when your pain is a direct consequence of you or your community's sin. I suggest you read all of Lamentations.

REFLECTION

Have you considered how stories, in so many ways, shape our core beliefs and composite identity? We each have a multitude of stories that make up our sense of who we are—ancestral stories, family of origin stories, cultural stories, trauma stories, and even the stories embedded in our nervous systems.[94] What painful part of your story (past or present) makes your heart cry, *God, why?!* Why is it important to take that question to God?

---

94 As trauma-informed licensed professional counselor K. J. Ramsey shares in her book *The Lord Is My Courage* (Grand Rapids, MI: Zondervan Reflective, 2022): "Often, our bodies are speaking what our minds are afraid to say, stories most of us have never had space to tell. The tales our bodies tell through our sensations reveal our deepest wounds, truths, and hopes," 27.

Speak, Please

When the sirens blast
and my ears ring
I can't hear a thing
covered in rubble
I grope for a familiar thing
stumble on cement instead
—speak to me
whisper my name
sit me down
and tell me your secrets
tell me you're mine
tell me I'm yours
tell me you know best
speak to me in a voice of
still, smallness
and I will rest
I will let tears pour into a river
and you will let it rain, together we'll
nourish trees of hope
green shoots undeniable in the gray of smoke.

How We Got Here

Do not love the world or the things in the world.
If anyone loves the world, the love of the Father is not in him.
For all that is in the world—the desires of the flesh and the desires of the eyes
and pride of life—is not from the Father but is from the world.

I JOHN 2:15–16

Not all stories are best told with a linear plot. The key to feeling the weight of what was at stake during the time of the Davidic kings (1–2 Chron.; 1–2 Kings) is actually to start at the end: Judah's exile from the Promised Land by the hand of Babylon, which we read about yesterday. As God's people suffered the worst of the curses He promised them for their long-standing unfaithfulness (Deut. 28:15–68), what were they to make of His promises to Abraham, to Moses, to David? What were they to make of Him?

So now, let's rewind time about 384 years from Judah's deportation to the shining moment of David's heir, King Solomon: the dedication of the temple built for Yahweh, an Eden-like throne for the true King of Israel. God's glory descended as physical proof of His ongoing commitment to live with His people. And Solomon prayed a most beautiful prayer—beginning and ending with his utter trust in God's steadfast love and filled with requests for God to forgive His people when they strayed (2 Chron. 6:14, 42; cf. Ex. 34:6–9).

Yes, "the LORD loved him" (2 Sam. 12:24) and Solomon "loved the LORD" (1 Kings 3:3). But Solomon also "loved many foreign women" (1 Kings

11:1) who turned his heart toward their Yahweh-opposing gods. Solomon abused his power, breaking all the commands for kings God laid out in His law of love (Deut. 17:14–20)—acquiring excess wealth and many wives, making political-religious alliances with Egypt, and using forced labor. Yet his reign was considered the golden age of Israel, when "Judah and Israel were as many as the sand by the sea. They ate and drank and were happy," and, "Solomon ruled over all the kingdoms from the Euphrates to the land of the Philistines and to the border of Egypt" (1 Kings 4:20–21). These were the days of promises fulfilled—specific promises made to Abraham now finally tangible in the Promised Land (Gen. 15:18; 22:17). The best of times, right?

Though they ate and drank without lack, the foundation of their kingdom had cracks. Their covenant representative (the king) was found lacking, caught between his love for God and his love for the things God opposed. Solomon's double-minded kind of love had a generational effect. Pet sins, after all, morph into monsters. After his reign, the kingdom split— cutting off Israel (north) from Judah (south), leading to institutionalized idolatry in Israel and even in Judah (where the temple was). The Davidic dynasty progressed in Judah, but with regard to love for God and neighbor, it truly *regressed* into bolder idolatry and injustice.

REFLECTION

There's a difference between getting settled and settling. Because God's love is so lavish, do you presume that what you do here and now doesn't really matter? Do you forget our relationship with God is never nourished by our sin? Will you keep chasing lesser lovers, becoming, in the end, just like them—a lesser lover?

A Year with No Storms[95]

A year with no storms
brought forth a crop
different than the year before.
The fruit seemed healthy
bright, alive with color
but once bitten into
lacked nutrients, and its seeds
were mysteriously missing.
And even the trees
seemed stronger with thick trunks
but their trunks, when knocked upon
sounded strangely hollow,
their branches stretched wide
but roots were skinnier
less firmly gripping the drying soil
less deeply pressed into the ground
     below.
And the pond was a deep blue,
sparkling, but shallower than before
less fish found a home in its
once-transparent skin.
The grass was finally greener
and upon it the flock grazed
somehow unable to relate
to those skinnier sheep
in the other tempest-stricken pasture.
And the people, you see,
had more than enough to eat
their belt buckles were bursting
holding back the fat of prosperity

They were laughing, happy
at their feasts, their houses intact
and hands uncalloused from that
stormless year . . .
But a creeping
     weight
          sat upon their chests
          as they reclined at night
     causing them to sigh
before falling asleep again.

---

95 A poem-in-conversation with Ernest Hemingway's short story "The Snows of Kilimanjaro" (*Esquire Magazine*: August 1936).

The Prophets' Cry: Love's Longing in the Land

What shall I do with you, O Ephraim?
What shall I do with you, O Judah?
Your love is like a morning cloud,
like the dew that goes early away. . . .
I desire steadfast love and not sacrifice,
the knowledge of God rather than burnt offerings.
But like Adam they transgressed the covenant;
there they dealt faithlessly with me.

HOSEA 6:4, 6–7

When you experience a major betrayal—from a lover, friend, co-worker, family member, spiritual leader, someone you have genuinely loved—don't you feel both a fury at the violation *and* an unrelenting wish for restoration? Don't those waves of grief spin you 'til dizzy with a deep regret for how things turned out? Isn't this a mini hell—disunity you were never created for? Have you ever considered that this inexplicable emotional pain is an echo of what Brennan Manning called "the furious longing of God"[96]—that deep desire of God to be known and loved by His own beloved, and for His beloved to know the depth of His love for them?

We've explored the (apparent) end of God's promises at Judah's exile, as well as the beginning of Israel's golden age under King Solomon. But in

---

96 Brennan Manning, *The Furious Longing of God* (Colorado Springs, CO: David C Cook, 2009.

between was the corruption of love—from the Israelite and Judean kings (Ezek. 34), to the greedy priests (Mic. 3:11), to the false prophets who promised peace in the face of the people's spiritual adultery (Jer. 6:14). They bowed to their neighbors' gods (Egypt, Assyria, Babylon—their "lovers," as God put it) hoping for military protection. Hear the cry of children sacrificed on the altars of false gods, migrants robbed on the highways of trade, the poor calling for justice to no avail. Watch as God's people participate in praise services, as if they don't reek of injustice and infidelity (Amos 5; Isa. 58).

But love never lets us stray without a faithful witness. It cries out in the wilderness of our wandering hearts. Yes, love had a voice in those generations: the prophets who persistently proclaimed Love's (God's) longing in the land. What's Love's longing? To be fully known and fully loved—the same need we each have, inflamed with pain when our inherent dignity is transgressed. The same furious longing you'll find in a husband scorned by his adulterous wife (Hosea; Ezek. 16), a father dishonored by his beloved son (Jer. 3; Mal.1), a mother who yearns for her rebellious children (Isa. 66:13; cf. Matt. 23:37), a friend slandered and rejected (Isa. 40–41). Through the prophets, God's soul cried: "Return!" "Know Me!" "Seek Me sincerely!" But the faithful were few. And the voice of the prophets—Love's cry—was all but muted.

REFLECTION

Do you hear Love's cry for you today? Will you let your longing to be known and loved lead you to God's longing for the same?

The Prophets' Vision:
Look Back, Look Forward

I have loved you with an everlasting love;
therefore I have continued my faithfulness to you.

JEREMIAH 31:3

Not all stories are best told with a steady progression from beginning, to middle, to end. The prophets sometimes spoke of present realities, sometimes the past, sometimes about future promises, and sometimes a mix. Maybe there's something to say about their not conforming to our modern, Western approach of chronological storytelling—like how God's core nature (*hesed*) stays the same "yesterday and today and forever" (Heb. 13:8), no matter the place we find ourselves in His story. The prophets' vision was always backward and forward, even at the same time. Their role was to call God's people to look back *and* to look forward.

His people needed to look back at the Mosaic law to remember His great love for them in their story. Their story was their identity—a people rescued and ruled by a God "abounding in steadfast love" (Ex. 34:6). Looking back would allow them to move forward in faithful love.

But the prophets also called God's people to look forward to God's "new covenant" (Jer. 31:31)—the final covenant in His epic love story. One that would encompass all those other covenants He made with Noah, Abraham, and David. God would write His law of love—the Mosaic law they broke—"on their hearts" (Jer. 31:33). He would replant His scattered people in the Promised Land (Jer. 32:41; Isa. 40) and unite them under a

Davidic king they'd call Immanuel, which means "God with us" (Isa. 7:14), who would rule over a New Jerusalem (Zion) with justice and peace, making Israel a blessing to all the nations (Isa. 27; cf. Gen. 12:3). God would even punish Babylon—that archetypal empire of all things anti-love (Isa. 13–23). He would "swallow up death forever" and "wipe away tears from all faces" (Isa. 25:8). But how? Through God's chosen servant (Isa. 42)—the true "Israel" (Isa. 49:3)—who, like the prophets before Him, would suffer oppression (Isa. 53). But His death would be unique. He would be "pierced for our transgressions" (Isa. 53:5), and yet, after death, "prolong his days," sharing the reward of His sufferings with many (Isa. 53:10).

God's people would experience exile, life as refugees in foreign lands,[97] and for some, a return to Jerusalem and a less-glorious temple.[98] How would they continue to hope in God's plan of global restoration when their story, and all God's promises, seemed to have ended? Through faith in God's steadfast love (Lam. 3:21–26)—a love He promised would never, ever end.

Today, we live under the new covenant of the Messiah Jesus in fulfillment of what the prophets proclaimed (1 Peter 1:10–12). But not all the promises have been fully fulfilled yet. We still die, cry, and sin as we live in evil empires like Babylon. But if there's one thing the prophets teach us it's this: it matters how we respond to God's love in the present. How we participate in the love story God has written depends on how we choose to look back *and* look forward—whether by faithlessness or faith, as scoffing spectators or persevering participants.

Reflection

If God's love isn't bound by time, why does it matter how we respond to His love here and now?

---

97 See the books of Daniel and Esther.

98 Post-exilic prophets who spoke as God returned them: Haggai, Zechariah, Ezra, Nehemiah, Malachi.

A Loving Author, Unresolved Subplots

Remember my affliction and my wanderings . . .
My soul continually remembers it
and is bowed down within me.
But this I call to mind,
and therefore I have hope:
The steadfast love of the LORD never ceases;
his mercies never come to an end.

LAMENTATIONS 3:19–22

Maybe you already know your life is a story, and a redemptive one at that. But then, what of all the stories within your story that still have loose ends? All those subplots of your family's generational sin, those relational fallouts that still don't make sense, those tragedies within the supposedly victorious epic that is your life's story in Christ? If you're like me, you've groaned: *I just want to forget it all.* And maybe you try to. Christians can sometimes be expert denialists—spiritually bypassing their pain with Bible-verse Band-Aids and pithy phrases as forms of emotional avoidance. But scars don't move; they cement into you. How can we engage our past and present pain with great hope, and not avoidance?

There's a looking back, like Lot's wife (Gen. 19:26), that is dangerous: longing for the ways of corruption God is trying to rescue us from. There's a "forgetting what lies behind" (Phil. 3:13) that is necessary for our endurance:

divesting from the sins that ensnare us. But we're sorely mistaken if we think this means we are to never engage our story's past—its themes, cycles, victories, *and* tragedies. Suppression of your emotions is not next to godliness. Honesty is. It's because of our great hope in the love epic's ultimate end, we of all people should be the most willing to lament our stories' brokenness.

This is what the author of Lamentations does as he circles a decimated Jerusalem, beholding the sickening wreckage of the temple, the Davidic king, the tablets containing the Mosaic law—all these redemptive themes in God's story . . . gone. The prophet doesn't rush past the tragedy. He "continually remembers it." He spends the front and back end of his proclamation picking up every broken shard and examining it with great grief. It's because he's willing to sit with the brokenness that he can cling with his whole heart to the promise: "The steadfast love of the LORD never ceases." *This* is his hope, even though he presently feels hopeless (Lam. 3:18). He knew their story wasn't over because God's love wasn't over.

There are some subplots God keeps unresolved—prayers you don't see answered, relationships you don't see reconciled, diseases you don't see healed. So you *must* grieve, you *must* weep, and you *must* look back at past wounds and lament. It's in that soul honesty where the loving Author of history meets you on the floor and writes the sort of resolution you perhaps didn't expect: a resolution that supersedes, for now, your circumstances. A resolution that develops your character through years of letdowns and unresolved conflict. A resolution in your soul: *God's love isn't over, so neither is my story.*

REFLECTION

What are some ways the story of Scripture is reframing or reshaping your understanding of your own story and identity?

You Stay

It was her first time on the baby swing
(my friend's third baby)
so I whipped out my phone
to record this milestone
some token to remember this day
(with my friend's third baby)
she's the same age I had
imagined my second would be
by now—
instead, I felt my ovaries cramping
again.
a shooting pain
enough to send me limping back
to my car for some Motrin
four orange useless pills
to remind me
my body rejects
my heart's longing.

Six months ago I heard
the word I'd often given thanks
I "at least" didn't have:
    "Endometriosis. Stage 4."
with surgery wounds yet
to harden and darken,
I already knew but asked,
    "What can I do?"
    "Nothing, really. Just keep eating
        healthy."
I already knew but Googled:
    "It's a disease shrouded in mystery
    even after surgery and pills
    it can worsen still."

I already knew but searched:
    "Endo belly is real, a cruel irony—
    looking pregnant
    while unable to conceive."
I already knew
you don't owe me my "Why?"
already knew
I can't imagine your plans
already knew
I should trust your heart,
but every month I'm plunged
into a bottomless pool
I breathe in water as air
and wonder
where you are
and
why
why
why.

I recently heard:
my deepest anguish—that's where
you dwell.

I imagine you crouched
in a dark, cold cave
gently holding the fragments
of my shattered dream
your eyes wet as the miry floor
your body heaving
something deeper than sympathy
you don't rush out
change the subject

or ask, "Have you tried . . . ?"
you stay.

you place your pierced hand
on every shard
examining every sharp edge
that has pierced me.
the lacerations on my belly
have now scarred,
but not my heart.
you stay.
so long as this wound festers
you stay.
'til, one day,
I'll hear you loud:
    "Quina! Come out!"

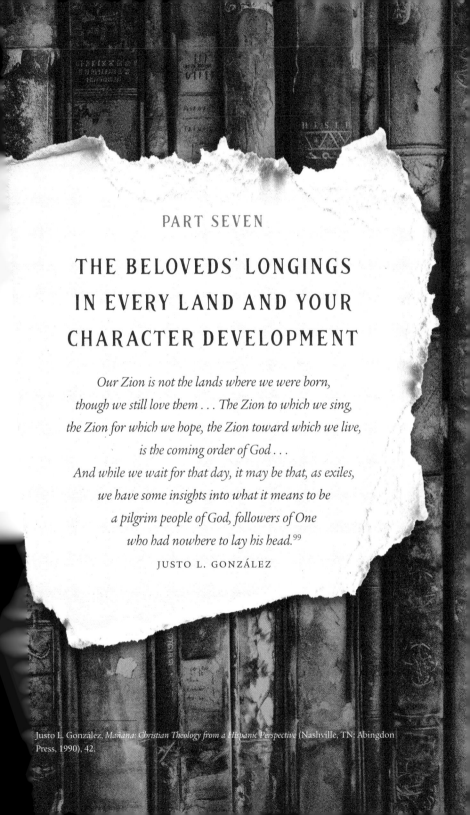

PART SEVEN

THE BELOVEDS' LONGINGS
IN EVERY LAND AND YOUR
CHARACTER DEVELOPMENT

Our Zion is not the lands where we were born,
though we still love them . . . The Zion to which we sing,
the Zion for which we hope, the Zion toward which we live,
is the coming order of God . . .
And while we wait for that day, it may be that, as exiles,
we have some insights into what it means to be
a pilgrim people of God, followers of One
who had nowhere to lay his head.[99]

JUSTO L. GONZÁLEZ

Justo L. González, *Mañana: Christian Theology from a Hispanic Perspective* (Nashville, TN: Abingdon Press, 1990), 42.

You Think We're Just Singing

You think we're just singing.

    we're fighting

        flanking our fear

        breaking the teeth

        of our unbelief

    till doubt is dead

        and all rebellious spirits and flesh

        find their necks

        under the heel of our

        conquering King.

But you think we're just singing.

Singing 'Til
Love Leads Us Home

By the waters of Babylon,
there we sat down and wept,
when we remembered Zion. . . .
How shall we sing the LORD's song
in a foreign land?

PSALM 137:1, 4

While in exile in foreign lands, like Babylon, Yahweh's people felt cut off from their own story, their own sense of identity as His—no temple, no Davidic king (*messiah*), and no tablets of the law. Yet, love always has a witness. The prophets spoke God's Word to His people, and God acted on their behalf to preserve them (see Daniel and Esther). Then, in the days of Ezra and Nehemiah, when Babylon was overtaken by Persia, God kept His promise to bring His people back to the Promised Land (Isa. 40; Jer. 25). What God revealed to Moses held true: His steadfast love lasts longer than His anger (Ex. 34:6–7; Neh. 9:17).

The returned exiles rebuilt the temple and city walls. Ezra taught the *Torah* (the Mosaic law)[100] to them and led them in an emotional covenant renewal ceremony (Neh. 8)—like a vow renewal between a historically

---

100 The Hebrew word *Torah* (often referring to the first five books of the Bible) is translated in English as "law," but it can also mean "instruction." Israel's God-given instructions (*Torah*) were not just legal codes but the story of their origin and redemption.

adulterous bride and her faithful Husband. But not all of Yahweh's promises had come to pass (Ezra 9:8–9), and the glory of this second temple didn't compare to Solomon's (Ezra 3).

It's during this post-exilic time, as God's people struggled to understand and embrace their story and identity, that the Psalms were most likely collected and organized into five books by scribes guided by the Holy Spirit.[101] Psalm 1 gives us the purpose of the whole thing: "Blessed is the one . . . who meditates on [God's *Torah*] day and night" (Ps. 1:1–2 NIV). The Psalms are a collection of poems and songs that gave instruction (*torah*) to God's beloved people so they could live a life of blessedness under the reign of Yahweh, regardless of their circumstance.

Maybe you've heard, "God has a wonderful plan for your life." True enough. Yet, we struggle as "exiles" in this life (1 Peter 2:11), homesick for Zion—the new Jerusalem (Heb. 12:22; Rev. 21:2). What of the murdered prophets of today, God's people stuck in poverty, the persecution of our brothers and sisters? What are you to make of your story and identity, and God's story and identity, when your health, your relationships, your emotions, all seem to suggest anything but the love of God? The Psalms tell us: we sing.

We sing *because* we believe, and sometimes we sing *until* we believe. Together, we worship—whether by hymn, praising God for His work in history, and when life is going well; or lament, crying to God in the painful darkness; or thanksgiving, praising God for what He's done for you personally.[102] The whole kaleidoscope of human experiences and emotions are found here. The Psalms reflect our longings and shape our souls as God's beloved people, wherever we find ourselves in the story . . . singing 'til Love leads us home.

---

101   The five books of the Psalms mimic the organization of Torah ("instruction")—the Bible's first five books (Pentateuch).

102   I borrow these three categories of psalms from the *Help Me Teach the Bible* podcast episode titled "Mark Futato on Teaching the Psalms," The Gospel Coalition, March 8, 2018, https://www.the gospelcoalition.org/podcasts/help-me-teach-the-bible/mark-futato-teaching-psalms/.

Tell me, beloved, the cares of your heart.
Oh, where do I start?
Right where you are.

Transformed by Love
While Praying the Psalms

Trust in him at all times, O people;
pour out your heart before him;
God is a refuge for us.

PSALM 62:8

When I'm too overwhelmed to pray aloud, I sometimes draw a huge heart on a page of my journal. Above the heart, I write out today's passage. Inside the heart, I jot down the ways I'm hurting, scared, angry, filled with shame, and so on. I offer this heart, my heart, to God in prayer—expounding on those bullet-pointed things or, so overwhelmed, just pointing to the page and saying, "God, here. Please, help." Sometimes the words won't escape my mouth, but the tears escape my eyes, each one a prayer splashing on that page. And I know God is near.

One of the many gifts of poetry is empathy—introducing us to our own emotions . . . and to God's. As my author friend Rich Pérez says, "I can be okay with a theology that tells me to be cautious with my emotions, but I can't be okay with a theology that tells me to not listen to them." The Psalms help us slow down the frantic pace of our lives and feel the emotions we might otherwise shame ourselves for or ignore. They teach us that because we're made in the image of the God who feels, we, too, should allow ourselves to feel whatever we're feeling and offer it to God with the Psalms as our guide. In this act, we experience God's love, which empathizes with *and* transforms our emotions.

But the Word of God is best experienced as a community treasure. As I listen to fellow believers pray or sing the Psalms, I find that those lines I can't quite connect with hit home for others. This creates a greater intimacy with God and each other, making it possible for us to "rejoice with those who rejoice," and "weep with those who weep" (Rom. 12:15)—often in the same sitting.

Praying the Psalms together knits our hearts as one, turning our emotions into telescopes through which we might better see and appreciate the emotional life of God. Jesus, the fulfillment of the "Anointed" One (*Messiah*) in Psalm 2, is the divine King we pray and sing the Psalms to. But He's also God's chosen "servant" (Isa. 42), who became "a man of sorrows and acquainted with grief" (Isa. 53:3). Jesus prayed and sang the Psalms, too—even on the cross (Matt. 27:46; cf. Ps. 22:1). So, as we pray and sing the Psalms, we allow God to touch our wounds—and He allows us to touch His, too. This is intimacy. This is love.

Reflection

Here's how I pray the Psalms with others. Together, read Psalm 62 (or another psalm) aloud. Then, discuss how it might've spoken to its original audience, as well as any imagery that sticks out to each of you. Then, everyone can share a prayer request in light of the psalm you just read: maybe there's an anxiety, a confession, or a feeling of gratitude that something in the psalm provokes. Last, each person is assigned his/her verse(s) to read aloud. Once that person reads those verses aloud, he/she then prays about those verses aloud, connecting his/her personal prayer with those verses and weaving in any prayer requests of the group.

To Cry and Not Say "Sorry"

I often oddly feel grateful
when I can access my grief
when tears flow freely
as I speak or think on painful
or beautiful things.

I know it's a sign of healing
of body and mind reconnecting
like lost lovers, separated by storm.

I know it means I've done the work
of stillness, silence, breathing
of acknowledging, validating, permitting
my rage, my self-loathing, my fear
my most primal feelings—
it's hard to sit with them
I always thought I should
hide at their sight
"Kill the beast!" I thought
but I've always ran
right back into their arms.
it's hard to sit with them
they've always needed to speak
but, silenced, they sought
refuge in my sinews,
my addictions, my overachieving—
I offer them a chair now, lean in
and I'm seeing
kindness cover me.

I suppose this is holy ground
sitting with my aches, my vices, my shame
it's divine work to see
these parts of me—

whole junctions of time, memories—
sewn slowly back together, gently
into a whole-r me
so I can feel, and not dissociate
think, and not fight, flee, or freeze

be with all of me
enough to say, "Ouch"
when it hurts
and be heard
by willing ears:
mine and the divine

enough to cry
and not say,
"Sorry."

The Psalms and Complex Relationships

Consider my affliction and my trouble,
and forgive all my sins.
Consider how many are my foes,
and with what violent hatred they hate me.

PSALM 25:18–19

Where do you tend to locate yourself in stories? When retelling your life stories, do you tend to cast yourself as either hero or victim? I love how the Psalms hold a tension of, "God, I've had integrity! What they're saying about me isn't right! It's not the whole story. Defend my cause!" And also, "God, you know how sinful I am, all the ways I've blown it, all my blind spots." Because both tend to be true. We don't get to only ever be the hero or victim. But we also don't have to only ever be the villain. The Psalms don't allow for such 2D simplifications when our lives are filled with 3D nuances.

There are times we are just horrible to others. We play the villain, and we need mercy (Ps. 51). There are times when we're violated. We're victimized, and we need justice (Ps. 10). Then there's the rest of our conflicts—some weird mix of our wounds, blind spots, sins . . . and the other person's too (Ps. 25). As much as I wish others would hold space for my story, wounds, blind spots, and nuances, it's difficult for me to hold that same space for theirs. It's easier for me to rush into broad-brushed conclusions about their character. The Golden Rule is hard (Matt. 7:12).

I like that the Psalms hold all that space I long for and all that space I struggle to hold. We each desire to be seen, heard, delighted in, believed the best about, empathized with, and honored. We each want the other to walk in our shoes and choose compassion. Because the alternative—suspicion and shame—is miserable.

There's a shame cast on you when you've been willing to hold space for another's nuanced perspective, but they haven't done the same for you. When you can see why they're hurt, but they still can't see *you*—just a caricature, which they now believe (and worse, share with others). Where to hide but the cross? What to pray but the Psalms?

REFLECTION

When you read Scripture's stories and poems, notice which characters you tend to see yourself in most. Ask yourself, *Why do I see myself most in this person? What role does this person play in the story? What are his/her strengths and weaknesses, joys and pains, core questions and assumptions? What might that say about me?* Then reread the story, putting yourself in a different character's shoes—perhaps a character you least like or least relate to. Ask the same questions about that person. What does this exercise reveal about you, those you tend to love, and those you find difficult to love? How might this help you pray more specifically as you navigate the complexities of your relationships?

When Angry (A Recipe for Empathy)

Serving size
you and y'all
   (all)

Ingredients
walking, then
slow belly breaths
     (sitting on the ground is best)

Prep Time
as long as you need:
    breathe.

Instructions
1. Are you breathing?
2. Prep for curiosity: *behind my anger,*
    what's making me scared?
       not belonging? not having enough?
       that nagging suspicion I'm not
       worth love?

3. Increase heat: acknowledge the feelings
    behind your rage.
       This situation makes me afraid
       that (fill in the blank).

4. Let simmer: validate each fear with
    permission to feel it.
       I'm allowed to feel afraid that I'm
       not valuable / unloved / unseen /
       misunderstood / unbelieved . . .

5. Stir frequently: shh . . . selah, please.
      Notice the Spirit gently tending to
        every wound.
      Maybe pray something like,
      Holy Spirit, I invite you
      into this feeling of being afraid
      that (fill in the blank).

6. Taste: empathize with the divine,
    who, feeling, feels pain.
      Maybe pray,
      Jesus, you know the taste
      of hunger, danger, bodily aches,
      damaged reputation, relational
        strains.
      You know what it's like to feel
      my fear's refrain.

7. Possible variations: some prefer to
    write or talk all this out.
      Listen to your body's cues.
      If writing or speaking about it is
      triggering you,
      try doing this silently, slow
        breathing on the floor.
      Inhale: 1, 2, 3, 4.
      Hold for 7. Exhale for 8.
      Hey, you're doing great.

Pictures of end product not included.
    But it'll look something like:
      feeling more human, less robot.
      healthier conversations.
      honest, transformative prayer.
      something like the slow-cook
        process
      of Philippians 3:10, that is,
      fellowshipping—walking
        (cooking?)
      hand-in-hand—with the Chef
        de Cuisine
      of love-driven emotional vitality.

Heard, chef?

A Prayer for When God's Love Feels Like Hate

All of my best friends despise me, and those I love have turned against me.

JOB 19:19 CSB

Darkness is my closest friend.

PSALM 88:18

Today I offer you a prayer based on the book of Job and the darkest lament in the Psalms (Ps. 88). I wrote this while I suffered in a four-year fight with stage-4 endometriosis, four major surgeries, the deportation of family members, the death of my grandmother (Mamita), extreme financial stress, unresolved chronic back pain, and the disintegration of a close friendship. Though I don't wish my struggles upon you, I offer this prayer as a companion to you in yours:

What I've wanted from You are answers—clarity, simplification, direction, precision—because the evils of our world and the traumas don't make sense to me. Your mysterious ways can be enraging. You answer prayer, then You don't. You protect Your people, then You don't. Yet You demand our allegiance? Your seeming randomness feels cruel, as though You delight in our confusion and misery. So I've wanted answers. I've wanted You to defend Your frustrating ways in court, because a case for a good God doesn't look so good. But there's a contradiction in my demand for answers. As I suffer so much loss, the people who harm me the most are the ones trying to offer simplifications:

"Just have faith, and it'll work out."

"Well, no one is good. We all deserve to suffer."

"Cheer up. Look at all God has done for you."

"Maybe you have some unconfessed sin."

"God always heals His children."

"God will open your womb. I know it."

The simplifications sting the most. They dismiss the depths of my grief, and they hold no space for the utter mystery of Your ways. They try to skip, jump, and run past the valley of deep darkness where You sometimes lead us—the valley where death still stings, where we can't see what You're doing, where we grasp for the slightest indication of Your rod and staff (Ps. 23). The pithy, precise prescriptions for my layered, complex pain are the most bitter of medicines. They're "miserable counselors" like Job's friends (Job 16:2).

God, I've wanted answers. And I've hated them. I've wanted clarity. And I've hated others' attempts at offering it. I've wanted a more simple God— one who doesn't wrap Himself in dark clouds (Ps. 18:11). But I've bristled at the boxes we've made for You.

I want what I don't want. I know not what I ask.
You are God, and I am not.

REFLECTION

Maybe today's meditation reflects how you've been feeling. If so, perhaps pray this with me today: *God, please, send me even the slightest breeze of Your love.*

A Prayer of Rage, Actually—A Confession

Have I outgrown faith?
Did mustard-seed me
slip between the cracks
of that invisible hand?
the cracks of his claims
too big for me to stand—
the salvation of the world
in the hands
of slave masters and charlatans,
the light of life inside rapists
and "just forgive, we're all a mess"
    messages.
claims like "everything has meaning"
when everything seems madness, random.
claims like "pray and God will move"
or he won't, we don't know,
"just pray according to his will,"
so you pray for things like healing
and faith and life and thriving
to see crack babies and the oppressed
condemned to cycles of death
you tell me to be thankful hell's not for me
but how can I sing with this survivor's guilt
the stench of smoke around me?
"God works in mysterious ways"
is the claim
so mysterious I've never seen him
have you?
so mysterious we fight wars and shoot up
    stores
because *we're correct, never them.*

it never ends but
"He's coming back" is the claim.
has the blood of the martyrs not
fertilized enough church-seeds?
have landslides and earthquakes
not shaken you up enough?
when is our misery enough?
we tremble and plaster pithy platitudes
("just have faith") as band-aids
on the glaring, gaping wounds
you inflict,
    or allow,
        or see from a distance,
            or use,
                or sleep on,
                    or abuse, it seems
I just want to be free
but I also want to see
    you
I'm dying to see
    you
I'M DYING, DO YOU SEE ME?
do you respond to angry calls
to "show me your glory"?
how do my finite hands
hold enough space for all these
mysteries?

has faith outgrown me?
will you still hold me?

Love Forms Us in the Darkness

If I say, "Surely the darkness shall cover me,
and the light about me be night,"
even the darkness is not dark to you;
the night is bright as the day,
for darkness is as light with you.
For you formed my inward parts;
you knitted me together in my mother's womb.
I praise you, for I am fearfully and wonderfully made. . . .
My frame was not hidden from you,
when I was being made in secret,
intricately woven in the depths of the earth.
Your eyes saw my unformed substance.

PSALM 139:11–16

There's a certainty we can feel in our darkest seasons of pain and mystery: *Surely the darkness will consume me.* Yet it's in our darkest night of the soul, where God seems anywhere but with us, when we discover the nature of God's love: it forms us *in* the darkness.

This is why the psalmist says, "For," in the phrase, "For you formed my inward parts." In verses 11 and 12, he's contrasting what *we perceive* in the darkness (*it's going to swallow me whole!*) versus what God sees in the darkness (*it's no threat to Him at all.*). Sure, the darkness doesn't scare God, but I'm scared to death! I can't see how a single good thing could come from this dark season! So why should this truth about God comfort me? The

213

psalmist says, "For." That means "because." "For you formed my inward parts; you knitted me together in my mother's womb. . . . My frame was not hidden from you when I was being made in secret."

Remember the creation story? "There was evening and there was morning," then—boom—a "day" is complete (Gen. 1:5, 8, 13, 19, 23, 31). Dark then light, chaos then order. That's the rhythm. Your own creation story began in literal, physical darkness (your mother's womb). There you were, hidden from the world—but not from God. In that darkness the Master Artist was actively working, weaving tendon and muscle, forming skeleton and soul. In that darkness, you didn't contribute a single thing but your need. Yet here you are now, formed into a whole human being. Take a look at your head, feet, and everything in between. *That* was formed in the darkness. You began in darkness, but you were not forgotten. Could you ever fathom what Love is forming in you right now—in the belly of your story's deepest darkness?

Dark then light. This rhythm continues in Scripture, especially at the story's climax. Love-in-the-flesh *became* sin for us (2 Cor. 5:21), carrying in His body all our sin and sorrow (Isa. 53:4), dying in a noonday darkness (Matt. 27:45). He was buried in the dark belly of the earth. But on the third day . . . well, let's just say, darkness is as light with Him. Your doubts, your fear, your shame, your pain—they're as big of a hindrance to God's love as was that grave.

REFLECTION

When have you been certain that your story, or God's love for you, was over? When did you realize you were wrong about that?

I will not neglect the pen

I will not neglect the pen
the ink grease is my cry
when demons silence
my throat
I'll choke out
confession and complaint
lay it down before you
    (they'll call it irreverent
    you'll call it faith)
'til I feel you
breathing on my sorry face
I'll fall asleep
in peace.

— *in the darkness You're for me. in the
darkness You'll form me.*

DAY 75

A Loving Author,
Your Character Development

Only goodness and faithful love will pursue me all the days of my life,
and I will dwell in the house of the LORD as long as I live.

PSALM 23:6 CSB

The Bible is a story about God *and* us; it's a story about God *with* us. Likewise, your story is meant to be a story about God with you. It's a story God wrote and yet *is writing* with you, giving you agency to coauthor with Him. So, what is this loving Author most focused on in your story?

The five-book organization of the Psalms gives us a clue.[103] Book 1, Psalms 1–41, establishes Yahweh as the world's King through His anointed one (*messiah*—King David, but later, *the Messiah Jesus*). Book 2, Psalms 42–72, is about how David's kingship was transferred to Solomon. Book 3, Psalms 73–89, gets darker with questions about God's love and its apparent absence. Book 4, Psalms 90–106, shows us how to live when our faith says one thing (Yahweh reigns!) but our circumstances say another. And Book 5, Psalms 107–150, shows us how faith in a loving God should be lived out practically in a world full of lovelessness. Despite what Israel experienced, the Author still had authority (*author-ity*) over their story, and He remained committed to a redemptive arc. Hence, the

---

103 I borrow these themes of the five books of the Psalms from the *Help Me Teach the Bible* podcast episode titled "Mark Futato on Teaching the Psalms," The Gospel Coalition, March 8, 2018, https://www.thegospelcoalition.org/podcasts/help-me-teach-the-bible/mark-futato-teaching-psalms/.

Psalms' frequent proclamation: "Yahweh reigns!"

Your story with God entails the same questions and cries of the Psalms, but also, the same end. You see, the last five psalms of Book 5, 146–150, are the glorious resolution of the story. These doxologies, songs of praise, say "Praise Yahweh!" again and again. They depict what it will be like when our faith finally meets sight: creation and society's vulnerable restored, warring governments and the persecuted resting in *shalom*. And we'll praise the King who's *always* been reigning. What does this teach us? As we sing God's story, we internalize it. We are transformed as we process our human realities with God through the act of worship.

It's possible to know *about God* and not be changed; it's impossible to *know God* and not be changed. You've likely seen how life's darkness doesn't always change people for the better. But it's your faith in the loving Author, expressed through active worship, that transforms you.

This is our loving Author's main aim in your story: your character development. However long His long game, God exposes your soul's woundedness, not to leave you in it but to achieve in you a depth of character you could've never achieved without Him.

Whatever chapter you find yourself in—whether in "the valley of deep darkness" or by "still waters" (Ps. 23)—you can direct your every ache and joy to Him in worship. As you do, you'll find His *hesed* (faithful love) chasing you down all your days. And in the end, you and "everything that has breath" (Ps. 150:6) will praise Him . . . finally, with no hindrance.

REFLECTION

Can you imagine worshiping God with no sin, doubt, despair, or distraction?

Oh, soul

didn't you know

when I said,

"I will yet praise Him"

God was listening?

Did you forget He blesses

beyond wine and grain

and a thousand pleasures?

That every loss and longing

and lack

in Him is

anointing?

    Olives knocked down

    washed, stripped

    crushed into paste

    poured out as oil to kiss

    head and face

    with

    purer joy in His.

— *olive oil*

PART EIGHT

LOVE'S VIOLENT, BEAUTIFUL CLIMAX

How merciful our God, who thus imparts
O'erflowing tides of joy to human hearts,
When wants and woes might be our righteous lot,
Our God forgetting, by our God forgot![104]

PHILLIS WHEATLEY

104 *Memoirs and Poems of Phillis Wheatley*, ed. Margaretta Matilda Odell (Boston, MA: Geo. W. Light, 1834), 53.

DAY 76

Love Was Writing (His)tory

[Jesus] said to them, "How foolish you are, and how slow to believe
all that the prophets have spoken! Wasn't it necessary for the Messiah to suffer these
things and enter into his glory?" Then beginning with Moses and all the Prophets,
he interpreted for them the things concerning himself in all the Scriptures.

LUKE 24:25–27 CSB

One of my favorite storytellers, Sandra Cisneros, observed that "real life stories rarely come to us complete."[105] We remember fragments of people and events, but the emotions we feel stay. Those pangs of unresolved tensions stick. Yet, there was a man from a small, insignificant town called Nazareth, who saw the Scriptures as a story about Himself—one with multiple themes and subplots all converging into His story. This Jew, born under Roman occupation, saw Himself as the very climax of Israel's plot, the fulfillment of the redemptive themes in Israel's story, and the inaugurator of God's global plan of new creation through Israel.

This controversial man from the lower class had the audacity to confront the Jewish aristocracy and official leaders (the Sadducees, the chief priests, and the high priest) who used the temple as their power turf rather than a place for the hurting to meet with God. He wasn't afraid to call Herod Antipas—that self-indulgent, violent, Roman-appointed "king of the Jews"—a "fox" (Luke 13:32). He even enraged the Pharisees—those unofficial leaders who were nevertheless cultural influencers who hoped their

---

105 Sandra Cisneros, *The House on Mango Street* (Houston, TX: Arte Público Press, 1984), Kindle, 2.

strict purity and ancestral codes could encourage God to finally fulfill His kingdom promises to Israel here on earth.

This "carpenter's son" (Matt. 13:55) became a traveling teacher-healer, designating twelve men of Israel—representing its twelve tribes—as His apostles (ambassadors of the king) to carry His message all around Israel. The message? "The time is fulfilled, and the kingdom of God has come near. Repent and believe the good news!" (Mark 1:15 csb). He believed history's climax—a greater exodus—was happening, and it was urgent that Israel respond accordingly.

Exile and foreign oppressors had been Israel's story for centuries. But now, the kingdom, and its Davidic king—the Anointed One, *Messiah*—was finally near. Near enough to touch (1 John 1:1). Near enough for ceremonially "unclean" lepers and bleeding women to *be touched* by holy, healing love. Near enough to attract and transform Jewish sellouts such as tax collectors, prostitutes, and Gentile (non-Jewish) worshipers. Near enough to raise the dead. But like all men, His days were like "a flower of the field" (Ps. 103:15)—blooming in brilliance for a brief three-year public ministry, then snuffed out by the wind of those who feared revolution. He died in His prime, Roman-execution style—a stripped-down exile outside of Jerusalem's city limits.

It's true, you know: "real life stories rarely come to us complete." A shameful cross could've easily been the "period" to His life sentence— another subplot unresolved in the tragic drama of world history. "But the steadfast love of the Lord" writes a different story; it's "from everlasting to everlasting" (Ps. 103:17). And so it goes: He ended death's sentence with a "comma," breaking both grammar conventions and human possibilities with a plot-twisting resurrection. His tomb was left empty because God's promises were not. Love was still writing (His)tory.

Period.

Hannah had her
    period
in cycles
like
infinite loops
of the same death
sentence: you
will never be a mom
    period.
are a barren stump
    period.
      always period.
never a comma.
    a period.
no exclamation.
But blood led Hannah
to worship, though wordless
her life His
    period.
Apparently periods aren't periods
in the hand of God,
life soon swam inside
and Hannah's song
echoed history's halls
and Mary's mouth, the Magnificat
filled the mother of Messiah
    he was a barren stump
    cut off before bloom
    no descendants, doomed
    to death sentence
      period.
    But on a bloody, barren tree
    became fruitful womb

birthing children
from every nation
filling the mouths
of would-be moms
with
a more magnificent song:
"By His blood
I am the mother
of many sons and daughters
By His blood
I am honored
both child and mother
    period."

Familiarity Bred Love

"He has helped his servant Israel,
in remembrance of his mercy,
as he spoke to our fathers,
to Abraham and to his offspring forever."

LUKE 1:54-55

The climax of history had come. And how did God bring about this most blessed of occasions? Through a scandal. A woman betrothed was found to be pregnant. (Who ever said the Bible was boring?) From Eve, to Sarah, to Rebekah, to Hannah, to Elizabeth, Scripture's story is filled with women who have no business being pregnant. Why is that? God kept proving there's nothing too hard for Him, but He was also weaving an important theme into His grand drama of history: socially unqualified women bringing forth life.

That theme found its climax when the angel told the virgin Mary:

"Do not be afraid, Mary, for you have found favor with God. And behold, you will conceive in your womb and bear a son, and you shall call his name Jesus. He will be great and will be called the Son of the Most High. And the Lord God will give to him the throne of his father David, and he will reign over the house of Jacob forever, and of his kingdom there will be no end." (Luke 1:30-33)

Her betrothed, Joseph, an unwealthy carpenter who could trace his lineage back to King David (Matt. 1:1-17), was called to assume legal

223

fatherhood of the baby by marrying Mary and naming the child Jesus, which means "Yahweh is salvation" because He would "save his people from their sins" (Matt. 1:21).

In his memoir, author Rich Pérez asks the question, "What if, instead of contempt, familiarity bred love?"[106] Mary's knowledge and love for the story God had been telling through her people's history was what led to her Magnificat—that beautiful song of thanksgiving in response to the privilege she had to house in her body the Son of God (Luke 1:46–55). The Psalms constantly say to "sing a new song" to God,[107] yet Mary's "new song" was really a reflection of old promises. It echoes Exodus 15, Psalm 103, and, incredibly, Hannah's song (1 Sam. 2:1–10). Mary's familiarity with the promises God made to Abraham, repeated to Jacob, and expanded to David, filled her mouth with overflowing praise. She would get to birth the promised offspring of Eve: the serpent crusher (Gen. 3:15)!

Through her consenting body would come a never-before-done kind of conception. The Holy Spirit, as at creation, would create life in the darkness of her womb, and out would come the eternal, never-created Son of God—now forever tied to humanity as Mary's son. God's love was more than fuzzy feelings but historical promises kept in real time—swimming in her belly. And so, she sang.

REFLECTION

How might familiarity with the Old Testament story breed a greater love for the New Testament story? Why do you think it's important for us to learn, study, sing, and internalize the promises of God in Scripture?

---

106 Rich Pérez, *Mi Casa Uptown: Learning to Love Again* (Nashville, TN: B&H Publishing Group, 2017).
107 Psalms 33, 96, 98, 144, 149.

But Proximity to the Truth
Is Not Enough[108]

Now the goal of our instruction is love that comes from a pure heart,
a good conscience, and a sincere faith.

I TIMOTHY 1:5 CSB

Scripture's story is filled with irony. As Matthew emphasizes in his account that Jesus is the promised Messiah (the Christ) by virtue of His Scripture-fulfilling birthplace of Bethlehem, he also introduces his Jewish audience to a mysterious group of Gentiles: Magi from the East (Matt. 2). Look at the Christ child already causing the nations to "rally to him" (Isa. 11:10 NIV; 60:1–6)! The love of God is a scandal. It makes Christ worshipers out of pagans, faith heroes out of foreigners. But perhaps more shocking are those who use it to abuse, or simply yawn.

The Magi, this migrant caravan of Gentiles (non-Jews), entered Jerusalem—the center of Jewish religious life and the residence of Herod the Great, so-called king of the Jews—to find and worship the *true* "king of the Jews" (Matt. 2:2). The irony is almost laughable, until we see Herod's faux worship result in the slaughter of toddlers. Never underestimate the lengths some people will go to maintain their status and power—even some who claim to worship Christ. Christian celebrities or spiritual leaders may

---

108 This meditation is a revision of my devotional "A Disruptive Joy," ChristianityToday.com, December 16, 2020, https://www.christianitytoday.com/ct/2020/november-web-only/advent-week-4-savior-is-born.html.

have exploited and silenced you, and politicians may have weaponized the Word to diminish your dignity. But the "king of the Jews" is also the "King of kings" (Rev. 19:16). He will hold all wielders-of-power—those lowercase kings—into account. It's a part of the story, even if you don't see it yet.

But there's also a critical contrast between the Magi's response of worship and the apparent inaction of the chief priests and scribes. How could the Magi (Gentiles), Mary (a woman), and shepherds (the poor; Luke 2:8–20) receive the news of the Messiah-King's coming with songs and shouts and swift action, but these educated men couldn't be bothered to bow? To borrow a phrase from my husband, "proximity to the truth is not enough."[109]

We ache as we watch friends and family hear of God's love for them in Christ . . . and yawn, or scoff, or twist it for personal gain, or just distract themselves with every worry and pleasure under the sun. The whole point of Scripture's story is to birth in us "love that comes from a pure heart." But sometimes, people's familiarity with the Bible or church breeds contempt instead.

We must hold space for the nuance of discouraged hearts, worn down by oppression (see Ex. 6:9). But we must also choose the Magi's way— seeking "the bright morning star" (Rev. 22:16) with a sincere faith, even when our love for Him seems silly, subversive, or scandalous.

REFLECTION

Why is mere knowledge of God's Word not the gold standard for true faith in Him?

---

109 Jon Aragon, "Proximity to the Truth Is Not Enough," sermon preached on December 9, 2018, https://livingbyfaith.us/media/jjshrhr/proximity-to-truth-is-not-enough.

Love Embodied, Literally

And the Word (Christ) became flesh (human, incarnate)
and tabernacled (fixed His tent of flesh, lived awhile) among us;
and we [actually] saw His glory (His honor, His majesty),
such glory as an only begotten son receives from his father,
full of grace (favor, loving-kindness) and truth.

JOHN 1:14 AMPC[110]

We began this book with a reflection on the Father, Son, and Spirit—the "triune Community-of-Love"—existing in a diverse yet perfectly unified relationship before creation. Maybe that felt like trying to run before you could walk. But this is how the fisherman-turned-apostle John begins his story. John highlights the nature of "the Word" of God as One who "was with God" and who "was God" (John 1:1)—distinct yet the same, diverse yet unified. John then echoes the creation story, saying this "Word" is "life" and "light," the agent of creation. But then John shifts His focus to something completely new in Scripture's storyline: "And the Word became flesh and [tabernacled] among us" (John 1:14).

God became a real human in history. Just as God's glory came down to dwell in the tabernacle tent to be with His tent-dwelling children in the wilderness, so now He came down to dwell with us in human flesh. What humility! What solidarity! John continues: "and we have seen his glory, glory as of the only Son from the Father." This "Word" is the "Son" of God

---

110 Amplified Bible, Classic Edition, Copyright © 1954, 1958, 1962, 1964, 1965, 1987 by The Lockman Foundation.

the Father. And what was this "glory" John and the others saw in Him?

Remember when Moses asked God: "Please show me your glory" (Ex. 33:18) and God did so by declaring His name, Yahweh (I AM)? God said His glory was this: "[I AM], [I AM], the compassionate and gracious God, slow to anger, abounding in love [*hesed*] and faithfulness, maintaining love to thousands, and forgiving wickedness, rebellion and sin" (Ex. 34:6-7 NIV). God's glory has *always* been His self-revealing, ever-present, overabundant, patient, forgiving, and just love. Love moves outward, seeking to bring others into its goodness—even if the seeking is costly.

Jesus would later say, "The hour has come for the Son of Man to be glorified" (John 12:23). Glorified how? By becoming like a grain of wheat that dies in the darkness of the earth in order to produce "much fruit" (John 12:24). Execution by a Roman cross was the most shameful way to die. It was gross. Yet Jesus saw it as His glory.

Theologian Justo L. González puts it beautifully: "God is being-for-others. This is what is meant by the central biblical affirmation that 'God is love' (1 John 1:8). To love is to be for others. . . . The glory of Jesus is the same as the glory of God: for-otherness, love."[111] This is why John can say Jesus' glory is that He's "full of grace and truth" (John 1:14)—which is to say, He's "abounding in love and faithfulness" (Ex. 34:6 NIV). Jesus *is* Yahweh. He is Love-in-the-flesh—love embodied, literally.

REFLECTION

> If the Son of God *became* a human—Love in the flesh—then what does this say about God's concern for the fullness of our humanity: our physical bodies, our social struggles, our relationships, as well as our souls?

---

111 Justo L. González, *Mañana: Christian Theology from a Hispanic Perspective* (Nashville, TN: Abingdon Press, 1990), 152, 154.

The Greatest Mystery (A Hymn)

Triune in all Your myst'ry
too great for me to grasp
The way You came too lofty
for me to understand

You changed my heart just like the wind
invisible yet I feel you

I trust You, Lord
for Your secrets left unseen
But this the greatest indeed

How is it that You chose me?
Who am I to be made clean?

Beloved Before Doing

After Jesus was baptized, He came up immediately out of the water;
and behold, the heavens were opened, and he (John) saw the Spirit of God
descending as a dove and lighting on Him (Jesus),
and behold, a voice from heaven said,
"This is My beloved Son, in whom I am well-pleased and delighted!"

MATTHEW 3:16–17 AMP[112]

Before creating, the Son of God dwelt in triune love. And now, before the work of His ministry, He's declared "beloved." Being before proving, beloved before doing. Imagine that.

Then imagine this: the moment you desperately asked Jesus to free you from your slavery to evil (*your* exodus), the voice of God boomed from heaven, "THIS IS MY BELOVED CHILD, IN WHOM I AM WELL PLEASED!"— a proud Dad beaming over His new creation (Luke 15; Eph. 1:3-6).

> Delighted in before you did
> a single thing for Him.
> Poetic, isn't it?

It helps to note that in Scripture's story, "the waters" (or "the sea") usually represent chaos, or even evil and judgment. At creation, God defeated chaos, the waters, by bringing order, harmony, and unity. God separated "the waters" (sky and sea; Gen. 1:6); but in the corrupt days of Noah, God

---

112 Amplified Bible by The Lockman Foundation, La Habra, CA 90631. All rights reserved.

un-separated the waters in judgment. Through the separated waters of the Red Sea, God redeemed His people away from slavery. Then God did it again at the Jordan River as they passed into the Eden-like Promised Land (new creation). It's here at the Jordan River where God sent the prophet John the Baptist to prepare Israel for her Messiah-King.

Of course, "the waters" are also mentioned *before* God began creating. "The Spirit of God was hovering"—like a mother bird—"over the surface of the waters" (Gen. 1:1). Then God spoke. Now, as Jesus arises from the waters, the Spirit is "descending as a dove" and the Father speaks again. Creation 2.0, the new creation, was coming.

All who desperately wanted to be freed from their slavery to evil were welcome to this "baptism of repentance" (Mark 1:4)—brought down into the waters (judgment), then back up. By faith in Yahweh—who *is* salvation (cf. Ex. 15:2; Matt. 1:21)—the waters of judgment could become a vehicle of salvation. God's way was "through the great waters" (Ps. 77:19), just like at the Red Sea crossing. The exodus 2.0, the greater redemption, was dawning.

Even more, anointing oil symbolized the Spirit empowering a person for a special task—like when David was anointed by the prophet Samuel (1 Sam. 16:3). Now Jesus, baptized by the prophet John, is identified as the Anointed One (*Messiah*) by the Spirit. He's called "beloved," which is what David's name means. King David 2.0 was arising.

But there was another baptism coming (Luke 12:50; Mark 10:38). The Messiah-King, anointed by a woman (Matt. 26:12), would dive into the dark waters of judgment for our corruption. But He wouldn't stay there—turning the waters of judgment (the cross) into a vehicle of salvation.

Poetic, isn't it?

REFLECTION

Ephesians 1:6 says that we who have trusted in Christ are "accepted in the Beloved" (NKJV). So what do you think is the first thing on Jesus' priority list for you today: to shore up every way you need to "get your act together," or to bask in the blessedness of your Father's delight?

("This is my beloved child, in whom I am well pleased.")

Perhaps you're in a chapter of life where it's best you step away from ministry activity—or at least, ministry as you've understood it—to tend to your emotional, mental, and/or physical wounds. How might the Father's declaration at Jesus' baptism reorient your understanding of what it means to be "used" by God? How might taking time—however long you need—to pursue healing and recovery become a path of discovery into God's unwavering love?

Fasting So We Could Feast

The Spirit immediately drove him out into the wilderness.
And he was in the wilderness forty days, being tempted by Satan.

MARK 1:12–13

Right after Jesus is declared God's "beloved Son" (Matt. 3:17) at His baptism, He is driven into the desert by the Spirit. But wasn't He the One God delighted in? How could forty days and nights without food or drink, in a terrifying wilderness with wild beasts, reveal God's love?

The children of Israel who passed through the waters of the Red Sea (a baptism), wondered the same thing. How could the God who declared, "Israel is my firstborn son" (Ex. 4:22) lead them into "the great and terrifying wilderness" (Deut. 8:15)? Despite God's miraculous provision, they preferred the familiarity of slavery in Egypt. Even Moses, their covenant representative, didn't taste the blessing of the Promised Land due to his own sin. Suffering brought out the worst in them in those forty years.

But did the abundance of Israel's kingdom united under Solomon bring out the best in them? As we've seen, their full bellies exposed their fattened hearts, unable to feel the sting of their idolatry. King Solomon, their covenant representative, typified this double-minded kind of love.

Way before them was a man made in God's image dwelling in a most delightful garden. This man felt that perhaps God's one restriction was evidence of his scarcity. As humanity's covenant representative, Adam forfeited the chance to eat from "the tree of life" (Gen. 3:24) *for us.*

Does God have something against food or eating? Of course not! Jesus' life was filled with feasting (Matt. 11:19). But Satan was tempting Jesus to shirk His script in God's drama: to suffer first, then to be exalted (Matt. 4:8–9). Adam had chosen the opposite. The heart behind temptation has always been a question of loyal love: to God or to Satan. Jesus—"tempted as we are" (Heb. 4:15)—was humanity's new covenant representative who made the right choice *for us*.

To be most like God is to live in the fullest expression of our humanity. We were made in the image of God, after all. The most human thing to be is godly. Jesus, who *is* the actual image of God (Col. 1:15), showed us this. His love *for God* meant exemplifying true humanity for us: loving God by obeying His Word. And His love *for us* meant He put our need for righteousness above His desire for food. He fasted so we could feast, a counterrevolution of trusting God *as* His sustenance (Matt. 4:4). He chose perfect obedience to God, so we non-obedient humans can be credited with His righteousness and eat from the tree of life forever with Him (Rev. 22:14).

Love *for God* and God's love *for us* found its perfect expression in Jesus. So how could those forty desert days *not* reveal God's love?

REFLECTION

How does Jesus show us the full glory of being human? How might remembering that Jesus was, and still is, fully human help us to become more godly?

Our Beloved Myths and the Kingdom He Gives

And he lifted up his eyes on his disciples, and said:
"Blessed are you who are poor, for yours is the kingdom of God."

LUKE 6:20

This is a book about Scripture's story invading ours. Our identities are shaped by our stories, and our stories are always informed by the society we live in—handed down to us by things like our history books, our political affiliations, and the media we all consume.

For example, some believe "America can do no wrong," or that their country is superior to all other nations in its history, morals, and cultural ethos. We know that is not true for the US, nor is it true for any nation. To maintain that myth we must make Jesus in *our* image—an exceptional guy who "made it" and, "If you work hard enough, with a bit of His help, you will too." (And if you don't socially advance, there must be something inherently wrong with you.) To maintain that myth, we must make Jesus merely "a man upstairs," our personal assistant who helps us achieve self-actualization. To maintain that myth, we must reject Jesus' kingdom.

Scripture, of course, promotes diligent work: "Whoever works his land will have plenty of bread, but he who follows worthless pursuits lacks sense" (Prov. 12:11). But it isn't blind to unjust systems that keep the poor in their poverty: "The fallow ground of the poor would yield much food, but it is swept away through injustice" (Prov. 13:23). If anyone understood this, it was your average Jew in Jesus' day, overly taxed by their colonizer Rome, just trying to survive. The core question for Jews in Jesus' time was this: how will we see the kingdom restored on earth? The way people answered this revealed their core myths—the stories that shaped them. The way Jesus answered this question revealed the true nature of God's kingdom.

Matthew, once a tax-collecting oppressor of his own people, depicts Jesus as a new Moses going up on the mountain to proclaim God's law of love (cf. Matt. 5; Ex. 20). The Sermon on the Mount revealed the identity and character of His kingdom participants: "Creator's blessing rests on the poor, the ones with broken spirits . . . on the ones who walk a trail of tears . . . on the ones who walk softly and in a humble manner . . . on the ones who are merciful and kind to others . . . on the pure of heart . . . on the ones who make peace . . . on the ones who are hunted down and mistreated for doing what is right."[113] Jesus was restoring the kingdom of God *through* Israel, as was always the plan (Gen. 12:3). But His kingdom would be an affront to every myth we love that exalts dominance above faithfulness (*hesed*).

Those who felt their heritage as Abraham's descendants meant their royal destiny was sealed? Those who winced at the thought of Gentiles being a part of this kingdom? Those who saw their social status as evidence of Creator's favor? Those who felt justified through their strict adherence to purity codes? Those who felt separation from the world proved their godliness? To them, this kingdom was offensive.

But the poor who heard this kingdom as a dignifying, liberating invitation rejoiced: *I can be freed from my hatred for my oppressors that consumes me?! From my constant worry about food and clothing?! From my fear of death?! I don't have to wait for society to change before I can experience this freedom?! This is good news!* The rich who heard this kingdom as freedom from the false security of wealth, and participation in the restoration of a just society (the new creation), laid down their possessions to follow Him (see Zacchaeus's story

113 Excerpts from Matthew 5:3–10, *First Nations Version: An Indigenous Translation of the New Testament* (Downers Grove, IL: InterVarsity Press, 2021).

in Luke 19). But, overall, it was "easier for a camel to go through the eye of a needle" (Matt. 19:24) than for the rich to receive it.

The heirs of this kingdom would come from every corner of society, but they'd all be shaped by the story of their King who chose poverty, oppression, and death to liberate them from evil's grip.

REFLECTION

Is this the love story that shapes your identity, taking shape in how you live? What are some ways we tend to double down on our society's myths and defend them even if they go against what Jesus said?

Lavish Love Befits the Forgiven

"Therefore I tell you, her many sins have been forgiven;
that's why she loved much. But the one who is forgiven little, loves little."

LUKE 7:47 CSB

Luke, the Gentile physician who wrote an account of Jesus, was not a comedian. But the last bit of Luke 7 reads like the beginning of a joke: a Pharisee, "a woman of the city" (Luke 7:37), and a prophet walk into a dinner party. Oh boy.

The Pharisee knew the prophet's reputation: He had cast out demons, healed the sick, and even—like the great prophet Elijah—raised the son of a widow from the dead (Luke 7:11–17; cf. 1 Kings 17). In Scripture's story, an explosion of miracles like that meant something massive was coming. It was an honor to host such a man! But this woman of shady reputation knew the prophet in a different way. She had a history with Him. Not the salacious kind she'd had with other men. He was different. So different she threw off all social conventions and worshiped at His feet—pouring out special ointment and tears and kisses, wiping them with her hair.

If that sounds strange, imagine how the Pharisee was feeling: "This man, if he were a prophet, would know who and what kind of woman this is who is touching him—she's a sinner!" (Luke 7:39[114]). But he didn't say this aloud, of course. So the prophet-in-question goes ahead and reads the Pharisee's mind for him: "Simon, I have something to say to you" (Luke 7:40). And He proceeds to tell a story.

---

114 References from this point through the end of this meditation are from the Christian Standard Bible.

The story is about a guy who owed two months' income to a creditor and another guy who owed twenty months' income. The creditor forgave both. "Now which of them will love him more?" (Luke 7:42) the prophet asks. The Pharisee answers as you and I would: "I suppose the one he forgave more" (Luke 7:43). And the prophet's like, "Exactly."

Now, this prophet wasn't exactly a comedian, but he was definitely clever. And the Pharisee was kind of like the guy in the crowd who gets singled out at a comedy show. The prophet tells the Pharisee to look at this woman. I mean, really *look at her*—not just as a sinner but as the Pharisee's role model. The Pharisee didn't even anoint the head of the prophet, but here this woman wasn't afraid to anoint His feet. Then the prophet drops what at first seems to be the punchline: "her many sins have been forgiven; that's why she loved much." When we know how much God has forgiven us, we become first-rate lovers, beacons of hospitality, even unrefined worshipers who make self-righteous religious folk squirm. "Praise from the upright is beautiful" (Ps. 33:1); love from the forgiven is a whole sermon.

But then the prophet takes it too far. He tells the woman, "Your sins are forgiven" (Luke 7:48). The best comedians are great storytellers. But this was no laughing matter. The prophet was saying He actually has the authority to forgive sins. Only God can do that! Because of a prophecy in Malachi (Mal. 4:5), many thought He was the reappearance of the prophet Elijah.

"But who do you say that I am?" this prophet would ask His closest friends (Luke 9:20). That's the most important question, isn't it? May we answer with our lips and, like this woman, with lavish love that befits the forgiven.

REFLECTION

How does this story show us the difference between entertaining someone and showing hospitality? What are some ways we can welcome Jesus into our lives with lavish love? See Matthew 25:31–46.

Keep Listening to the Beloved

Jesus took with him Peter and James and John,
and led them up a high mountain by themselves. And he was transfigured
before them, and his clothes became radiant, intensely white,
as no one on earth could bleach them. And there appeared to them Elijah
with Moses, and they were talking with Jesus.
And Peter said to Jesus, "Rabbi, it is good that we are here.
Let us make three tents, one for you and one for Moses and one for Elijah."
For he did not know what to say, for they were terrified.
And a cloud overshadowed them, and a voice came out of the cloud,
"This is my beloved Son; listen to him." And suddenly, looking around,
they no longer saw anyone with them but Jesus only.

MARK 9:2–8

A "disciple" is a student. But Jesus' teaching went beyond the classroom. He called His disciples to "follow me" (Matt. 4:19)—living with Him as He traveled around Galilee. They didn't know all they were getting into, but they were willing to leave the familiar for Him. But what was difficult to leave behind were their preconceived notions about the Messiah. After witnessing His ministry for some time, the disciples understood Him as what Peter confessed: "You are the Messiah" (Mark 8:29 CSB). Yes and amen! But the disciples still had some learning to do.

Between them and their Rabbi were two competing narratives about the nature and mission of the promised Messiah. Peter, like many Jews of his day, believed a Scripture-informed story that depicted Him conquering Israel's oppressors and establishing His throne in Jerusalem (Jer. 23:5–8). Jesus also believed a Scripture-informed story about the Messiah—one that required Him to suffer execution at the hands of religious leadership, then resurrect (Isa. 53). He required His followers to form their identity around His version of the story: cross and then crown. A hard pill to swallow. Jesus is such a patient teacher, though. He repeated this same lesson again and again on His way toward His execution in Jerusalem.

At His transfiguration, these conflicting Messiah narratives were addressed. Peter, afraid by the scene reminiscent of God's glory at Mount Sinai with Moses (Ex. 19–20, 33) and later, Elijah (1 Kings 19), suggests a gesture that equates Jesus with Moses and Elijah, who represent the Law and the Prophets—the whole Old Testament. But God the Father speaks: "This is my beloved Son; listen to him." Then, all that's left is Jesus. Not only was Jesus greater than Moses and Elijah, but the way He taught and fulfilled Scripture's story was the only narrative they needed to embrace. "Listen to him" (cf. Heb. 1:1–2). You might think after all this the disciples would embrace His version of the Messiah story, but they struggled with it for quite a while. Can't you relate?

When you first began following Jesus, you didn't understand it all at once. You just knew you needed Him. But discipleship is a journey, not a destination. Along the way, Jesus corrects our narratives about God, money, sexuality, success, and every aspect of our humanity. You'll sometimes struggle to embrace His Word. But Jesus loves His follower-students, all the way "to the end" (John 13:1). He knows He's not speaking into a void but rather a heart filled with layered stories and assumptions. So keep coming to Him, keep asking Him questions, keep wrestling with Him—and most of all, keep listening to Him. His version of the story is best.

What if so much of our identity struggles are really struggles with our stories—the ones we're told, implicitly and explicitly, and the ones we tell ourselves? What if the work of Christ was not merely to get us to heaven, but to tell us a story about God's love that would simultaneously dignify, challenge, and transform our own unique stories into beautifully diverse expressions of His love?

What were some assumptions you used to have about who Jesus is, or what following Him means? What challenged those assumptions for you?

What's the resurrection to a dream deferred?[115]

What's the resurrection
to a dream deferred?
will we see unanswered prayers
raised from the grave?
will dead hope levitate
from pockets of abyss
in our souls, as smoke
rises, transforms
before our eyes
into grander colors, sounds, shapes
we never could've thought to pray—
too glorious to imagine?
too much to contain?

will we never forget
all you DIDN'T do
with our earnest vows
and yet somehow
proclaim,
"He doeth all things well"?

---

115 A poem-in-conversation with Langston Hughes's poem "Harlem" from *The Collected Works of Langston Hughes*.

Dying to Raise His Friend

So, when he heard that Lazarus was ill, he stayed two days longer
in the place where he was. Then after this he said to the disciples,
"Let us go to Judea again."

JOHN 11:6-7

Jesus' public ministry was nearing its end. His disciples had seen Him show His authority over chaotic nature, spiritual forces of evil, diseases, and every effect of the curse on our corrupted world. But now Lazarus's sisters, Mary and Martha, sent messengers to Him: "Lord, he whom you love is ill" (John 11:3). When you receive that call that your loved one is inching toward death's door, you drop every plan, pack as fast as you can, and rush to pray over them, to hold their hand—and in Jesus' case, to heal His beloved friend as He had done for so many strangers. But when Jesus heard this news, He purposely stayed put. How could this be love?!

What could possibly justify His delay that led to Lazarus's death? Perhaps, like me, you've wondered this as you've seen loved ones slip into eternity despite your desperate pleas for God to intervene. Perhaps, like Martha and Mary, you've said, "Lord, if you had been here, my brother would not have died" (11:21, 32). Perhaps you've prayed: *Where were You, God?! How could You?!* And if you haven't, why not?

Sit with this: Jesus doesn't rebuke either sister for their angry, grief-filled lament directed at Him. In fact, when Jesus sees Mary weeping, He's "deeply moved" (John 11:33)—so angry at how death violated His friends.

Jesus revealed to Martha just before this: "I am the resurrection" (John 11:25)—another "I AM" statement that identified Him as Yahweh (I AM). Yet even though He knows He's about to display that truth, He's affected to His core by the way death takes away your breath, your dreams, how it ends your story. And Lazarus was more than a news report to Jesus. This was His beloved friend! And so, "Jesus wept" (John 11:35). The life giver, sustainer, and resurrector, with all power in His hands, looked at death . . . and wept.

He's "deeply moved again" (John 11:38) at His friend's tomb. But now He's had enough. For this reason He came, and for this reason He delayed in the first place: "Lazarus, come out!" (John 11:43 NIV). And there was His beloved friend, who had been dead for four days (enough to begin to rot), walking out as if he had only suffered a sneeze. Jesus loved His friends so much He delayed His coming so they'd see "the glory of God" (John 11:40) like never before. His delay felt like a denial of His love, but it was actually setting up a greater display of it. God's ways can be so frustratingly mysterious sometimes. But when He says He loves you, when He says you're His friend, He really means it.

In fact, Jesus knew the same Jews who wanted Him dead would hear the report of this and want to silence it by killing Him (John 11:45–57). He knew His display of love for His friends would lead to the warrant for His arrest. For Lazarus to be raised from the dead, Jesus knew *He* would have to die. Jesus wouldn't just look at death, He'd have to drink it down to the dregs. Yet, here was Love-in-the-flesh: dying to raise His friend.

REFLECTION

What griefs are you currently suffering? Silently sit with the fact that Jesus is "deeply moved" by your grief.

The True Meeting Place
of God and Man

And when he drew near and saw the city [Jerusalem], he wept over it. . . .
And he entered the temple and began to drive out those who sold,
saying to them, "It is written, 'My house shall be a house of prayer,'
but you have made it a den of robbers."

LUKE 19:41, 45–46

As we've seen, the temple (house of God) and the city (of God) are some of the biggest themes in Scripture's story. From the temple-garden of Eden, to the tent-tabernacle in the wilderness, to the temple in the Promised Land, God had always been obsessed with dwelling with His people. "You shall be my people, and I will be your God" (Jer. 30:22) is Scripture's repeated chorus.

But humanity was exiled from Eden. And, like Adam, Israel and Judah's kings refused to rule as God intended, so two major exiles occurred—Israel to Assyria, Judah to Babylon—leaving the temple and Jerusalem destroyed. Babylon became the prototype city of anti-God lovelessness. But the prophets were given visions of a new temple and a new Jerusalem (Zion). Persia overtook Babylon and allowed for the Jews to return to Jerusalem and rebuild the temple. But it didn't measure up to the glory of Solomon's temple. It was destroyed and restored again before Jesus came onto the scene. But by Jesus' time it was led by corrupt leaders drunk with power and devoid of the *hesed* (just love) that defines God's presence. God's special love for society's most vulnerable, so blatant in the Mosaic law, was buried under the temple leaders' religious activity and theological justifications (Mark 12:40).

As Jesus now drew near Jerusalem, He had every right to destroy the temple again. The majority of the Jews had rejected their Messiah, missing the ultimate climax of their story. A great judgment was coming because of this: around AD 70 the Romans would destroy the temple, and its leaders would be removed. Like at the Babylonian siege, children would starve and die. The carnage would be immense (Luke 21; 23:27–31). As He beheld this city filled with the people He had loved through centuries, He wept—not wishing for them to perish. Yahweh's nature hadn't changed. Full of *hesed*, Jesus preferred their repentance and restoration.

Then, just as the prophet Jeremiah had wept for His people while also calling out their immorality, Jesus entered the temple in His righteous anger against the religious leaders who had turned the meeting place of God and man into a corrupt business. As He drives out "those who sold" He quotes Jeremiah, referring to the temple as "My house." This was no subtle statement. After Jesus expelled the exploiters, "the blind and the lame came to him in the temple, and he healed them" (Matt. 21:14 CSB). The maligned and marginalized all drew near to Jesus—the true meeting place of God and man.

In Jesus, God "tabernacled" among us (John 1:14). "Destroy this temple, and in three days I will raise it up" (John 2:19), He had said. And so, the divided factions of Israel's corrupt leaders—e.g., the Herodians, the Sadducees, the Pharisees—now united with that exact intention.

REFLECTION

At no point in Israel's history did God excuse or shrug at their oppression of others. In fact, Israel's mistreatment of foreigners and the poor among them constituted God's greatest acts of judgment against them. What are ways people use the Bible's story to justify the very opposite of what God's love is meant to do? If Christ followers are now God's temple (Eph. 2:22), then what corruptions of love might Jesus be driving out of your life today?

A New Covenant of Self-Emptying Love

"This cup that is poured out for you is the new covenant in my blood."

LUKE 22:20

Christ, our Passover lamb, has been sacrificed.

I CORINTHIANS 5:7

On the night before His death, Jesus celebrated the Passover with His friends. The original Passover was when the enslaved children of Israel were spared the judgment of the tenth plague in Egypt—the death of every firstborn son—by obeying God's command to slaughter and eat the flesh of an innocent, spotless lamb as a substitute instead. When God saw the blood of the lamb on their doorposts, He passed over them in mercy. This Passover meal led into the great exodus (redemption), through the parted Red Sea (baptism), and toward the Promised Land (new creation). This was the climax of Scripture's story . . . until now. The greater exodus was beginning— liberation from the evil that has enslaved all creation since Adam.

But first, the King would wield His authority by washing the feces-encrusted feet of His subjects (John 13)—sovereignty expressed in self-giving service. At this Passover meal, Jesus said the bread was His body, given *for us*. The wine was "the new covenant" in His blood, poured out *for us*. This was the new and final covenant of Scripture's story, fulfilling all the previous ones. This covenant was the one the prophets said would come (Jer. 31), healing humanity's *hesed* problem—our inability to keep covenant with God.

With it was the forgiveness of sins and thus, the end of the sacrificial system.

As God instituted the Passover holiday just before the exodus happened, so Jesus instituted this new covenant meal just before the greater exodus began. "Do this in remembrance of me" (Luke 22:19)—a shared meal to participate in the special relationship He has with us. But this was Passover. Where was the sacrificial lamb?

After predicting Judas's betrayal, Peter's denial, and the abandonment He'd face by His closest friends, Jesus brought the disciples with Him to a familiar place. He called Peter, James, and John, the three who had witnessed His divine glory at His transfiguration, to see Him in His vulnerable weakness (cf. 2 Cor. 13:4). There He was crying, heaving, pleading with anxiety and grief that almost killed Him: "My Father, if it be possible, let this cup pass from me; nevertheless, not as I will, but as you will" (Matt. 26:39; cf. Mark 14:34). He struggled with the story He knew He must fulfill, but He submitted even this to God. Betrayed, arrested, and falsely accused in court, He could've called for legions of angels to avenge Him (Matt. 26:53). His words "I AM HE" had knocked down the soldiers for a moment (see John 18:6). Yet "like a lamb that is led to the slaughter. . . he opened not his mouth" (Isa. 53:7).

He was innocent, sinless, blameless, spotless. But not powerless. The omnipotent Son of God "did not consider equality with God as something to be exploited" (Phil. 2:6 csb). The psalmist once prayed, "Your unfailing love is better than life itself" (Ps. 63:3 nlt). Yet Christ loved us more than life itself. The sword of God's sovereign authority would be wielded in service to humanity. The love of God is His willing vulnerability, His self-emptying, even to the point of death—"poured out for you." Jesus said, "Let the Scriptures be fulfilled" (Mark 14:49), fully committed to His role in the love story: "the Lamb of God, who takes away the sin of the world" (John 1:29).

REFLECTION

Sit with those two words "for you." How does partaking in the new covenant meal—the Lord's Supper, communion—help us celebrate God's steadfast love for us in Christ?

God, Why?[116]

God, I know your m.o.
isn't really to reveal
all your "Because" to the "Why?"
of our inquiring, languished minds
"Why do the oppressed cry
with none to hear?"
"Why do those who bear your name
    abuse?"
"Why this trauma, too?"
"Why trauma at all?"
"Why do you hide behind silence?"

(*silence . . .*)

When some shrug and say,
"Well, no one is good. No one deserves
    grace."
is that really enough space to hold
the mysteries of faith,
our deepest soul pangs?
or might there be a reason why
the language of lament is littered
with doubts and despair and rage?
might the cry "Why?"
be a valid prayer
and not merely filth to confess
even if we know your answer would be
something akin
to teaching a newborn
quantum physics?

(*silence . . .*)

But what if it's worth it
to cry to the sky
and whimper, "Why?"
maybe there's grace in that question
a humanity we're meant to taste
when our lips fix to say,
"How can you be good with all this bad?"

(*silence . . .*)

Why seal our lips with anger at you
(which you already know)
then seal our souls with shame at our
    anger
(which you already know)?
Why pretend our satisfaction with
    debate-ready
arguments?
Why forsake the intimacy of honesty?
Why not shout into the abyss?

(*silence . . .*)

When The Answer Himself
was plunged into the deepest darkness
suspended by dangling flesh,
he cried into the silence,
"My God, my God, why have you
    forsaken me?"

and made
"God, why?"
a holy cry.

---

116 A poem-in-conversation with Shūsaku Endō's novel *Silence* (London: Peter Owen Publishers, 1969).

Love's Violent Climax

For while we were still weak, at the right time Christ died for the ungodly.
For one will scarcely die for a righteous person—though perhaps
for a good person one would dare even to die—but God shows his love for us
in that while we were still sinners, Christ died for us.

ROMANS 5:6–8

The Messiah had said, "Love your enemies and pray for those who persecute you" (Matt. 5:44). And now He took it upon Himself to fulfill His own law of love. He had been mocked, tortured, and now He hung naked and nailed onto a wooden cross. He prayed: "Father, forgive them, for they know not what they do" (Luke 23:34). Both Israel (the Jews) and the Romans (the Gentiles) had been blinded by their own corruption of love to understand they were playing the villain at the climax of history's drama. Their bloodthirsty cries typify what our sin demands: "Crucify, crucify him!" (Luke 23:21). Yet He prayed: "Father, forgive them." Scripture's story had already been filled with incredible moments of God's willfully vulnerable love. But never like this.

His crime was written above His head in pure irony: "Jesus of Nazareth, the King of the Jews" (John 19:19). Here was the promised Davidic Messiah-King of Israel, crowned with the curse (Matt. 27:29; cf. Gen. 3:18), bleeding on the throne they thought He deserved. Here was the true Israel, the Servant of God (Isa. 42–45), dragged out of Jerusalem, willfully experiencing the ultimate exile judgment—not for His sins but for theirs (Isa. 53:5). And not only for Israel's sins, but also "for the sins of the whole world"

(1 John 2:2). Through Him, Israel would become the light of the world, drawing Gentiles in to behold Yahweh's love (Isa. 51:4; cf. Matt. 27:54).

As His flesh was torn so was the curtain of the temple, "from top to bottom" (Matt. 27:51)—removing the barrier between God and humanity. In the midday darkness of God's judgment (Matt. 27:45), Jesus, the sinless one, *became sin* for us "so that in him we might become the righteousness of God" (2 Cor. 5:21). Our sin for His righteous record?! Truly, Jesus loved His enemies! Our loving God suffered in the hands of sinners, so sinners could forever rest in the scarred hands of a loving God.

But the cross wasn't merely the means of our personal salvation. God made His creation "very good" (Gen. 1:31) and He refused to discard His defiled masterpiece. He would fight *against* the serpent *for* His creation (Gen. 3:15). Jesus' ministry was a foretaste of the new creation He was and is making, bringing *shalom* to everything evil has birthed—chaotic nature, our decaying bodies, our broken relationships, *and* our sinful souls. On the cross He completed the mission His Father gave Him by absorbing all that evil, so it could no longer lay claim on His creation (Col. 2:15; 1 John 3:8). That's why Jesus could triumphantly shout, "It is finished!" with His final breath (John 19:30). In His apparent defeat, He was crushing the serpent's head.

But if He had stayed dead, this would've all been a mere moment in history. Scripture's story found its climax at the cross, but *not only at the cross*. Now began its greatest plot twist.

Black Sabbath

Perhaps this is the saddest day
in the disciples' lives
the day after tragedy
when trauma haunts the mind.

sit.

don't rush past this day, as if
God only ordained Sunday
and not the despair before it.

sit.
with terrified disciples
in their despondence

sit.
let God teach you lament
free you from faux comfort
the theology of Job's friends.

sit.
let the Sabbath rest of Jesus in tomb
remind you he rested
because "it is finished."
let today confront the ways
you assume God moves
to bless his beloved.

sit.
'til your soul's ripe to taste
the sweetness of Sunday.

Love's Beautiful Climax

Jesus said to her, "Woman, why are you weeping? Whom are you seeking?"
Supposing him to be the gardener, she said to him,
"Sir, if you have carried him away, tell me where you have laid him,
and I will take him away." Jesus said to her, "Mary."
She turned and said to him in Aramaic, "Rabboni!" (which means Teacher).

JOHN 20:15–16

The Author of life was executed, but He was really executing a plot twist. Stripped of His clothes, He was stripping every demonic force of its power. Publicly dishonored on a Roman cross, He was putting Satan "to open shame" like a defeated king paraded through Roman streets (Col. 2:15). Redemption came *through* His exile, blessing came *through* His being cursed (Gal. 3:13). And every promise of God in every covenant He had ever made found its "yes" and "amen" in the Messiah's resurrection (2 Cor. 1:20).

Jesus died on a Friday, then they laid Him in a tomb. On the Sabbath His dead body rested. Then on the third day, the women who were witnesses to His death became the first witnesses of His resurrection (Matt. 28; John 20). But He revealed Himself first to Mary Magdalene—a disciple once possessed by seven demons (Luke 8:2). She supposed Him to be the gardener. She was wrong; and she was right. He was indeed the second Adam, the greater gardener.

Then Jesus appeared to His disciples and over five hundred witnesses for forty days, teaching and feasting with them (Acts 1:3; 1 Cor. 15:6). Look at Him making breakfast for His friends on the beach shore, restoring and re-commissioning Peter, who had denied Him three times, with three chances to proclaim his love for Jesus again—Jesus not even naming the heinous sin Peter had committed (John 21; cf. Ps. 103:12; Mic. 7:19; 1 Cor. 13:7). Can you imagine the morning after your most shameful act of sin, waking up to Jesus making you breakfast in your kitchen? Can you imagine Him handing you a plate then leaning over the table, mercy in His eyes? Look at Him gently addressing Thomas's doubt (John 20). Can you imagine Him sitting next to you in your deepest anguish, inviting you to touch His wounds? Isn't this what faith is?

God is an expert at bringing life out of dark nothingness. A new creation dawned with the Sunday sunrise—initiated by the risen Christ. His new body was a new kind of humanity. Lazarus, who Jesus raised from the dead, would eventually die again. But Jesus wouldn't. He *is* the resurrection (John 11:25). He didn't just come back to life after being dead. Through His resurrection, Jesus defeated death itself! Scripture's story began in Eden, the overlap of heaven and earth. And now Christ secured a new Eden: the whole earth will overlap with heaven! He won't do away with creation. He doesn't despise our bodies. He will raise it all in incorruptible beauty with a glory that never fades away, just like Him. Hallelujah, hallelujah!

A disembodied existence in heaven isn't the end of your story. We, and all the believers in heaven, eagerly anticipate "the redemption of our bodies" and all creation (Rom. 8:23). And while we wait, we proclaim His historic resurrection, live in His resurrection power of holy love, and anticipate that great day when He returns to resurrect everything—when every chapter of our stories will be transformed into irrefutable chronicles of His conquering love.

Resurrection Hymn

Blessed be the God and Father of our Lord Jesus Christ!
According to his great mercy, he has caused us to be born again to a living hope
through the resurrection of Jesus Christ from the dead.
1 PETER 1:3

My hope cannot die
because my hope,
He's alive.

My hope cannot die
because my hope,
He's alive.

My hope cannot die
because my hope,
He's alive.

— hope is a Person.

Your dead shall live; their bodies shall rise.
    You who dwell in the dust, awake and sing for joy!
For your dew is a dew of light,
    and the earth will give birth to the dead.
ISAIAH 26:19

A Loving Author,
Your Story's Climax

"I tell you, there is joy before the angels of God over one sinner who repents."
LUKE 15:10

See what great love the Father has given us
that we should be called God's children—and we are!

1 JOHN 3:1 (CSB)

The disciples thought maybe now they would see the fulfillment of the
Messiah's kingdom in all its glory: "Lord, will you at this time restore
the kingdom to Israel?" (Acts 1:6). After the resurrection, they were still
struggling to understand Scripture's story as Jesus did.

So, before He ascended (went back up) to heaven as our exalted King,
Jesus refocused their concern. It's not that God's kingdom wouldn't ever be
fully realized. Jesus will return in His forever-human body to conclude the
epic saga with glory (Acts 1:11). But instead of restoring Israel's national
sovereignty as He did in the past, God wanted Israel—through those first
apostles and disciples—to become a light to the Gentiles (Isa. 42:6), spread-
ing the good news of King Jesus from Jerusalem to "to the end of the earth"
(Acts 1:8). History's climax had happened, but it wasn't the end of the story
God was telling. The Messiah wanted them to join in the telling, expanding
the Holy Land (like Eden) to the whole earth (Matt. 28:18–20).

The most important decision you'll ever make is the decision to follow
Jesus. The Holy Spirit changes your heart to want God enough to turn away
from a lifestyle of sin and toward a life with Him. You trust Jesus is the Son

of God whose death and resurrection grants you eternal relationship with God. You cry out to Christ to save you. And—glory to His name!—He does (Rom. 10:9–13). Whether you vividly or faintly remember it, that moment is when you're reconciled with God—no longer His enemy but His friend. You're justified: Christ's righteous record is credited to you. It's your own personal exodus—redeemed, bought by Christ's blood, from evil's oppressive rule over you. It's when you're adopted into the family of God, His beloved child. It's the first moment you receive God's forgiveness for every unloving thought, word, and deed. It's when eternal life, as Jesus defined it, begins for you—intimately knowing Him forever (John 17:3). This is your story's climax. But the climax is never the end of a story.

The climax is when the major conflict of a story is overcome—the victory that ensures future rest. It's the moment that turns a tragedy (sad ending) into a comedy (happy ending). The climax is where the "happily ever after" is secured but not yet fully experienced. Since Eden, God has been eager to partner with humanity in the love story He's telling. God is a storyteller who wants to continue telling a story of His love in and through you. He wants you to coauthor with Him—picking up the pen too. But, as we'll see, we can't do this without divine help. Still, this climax is worth heaven's most ecstatic celebration. And certainly ours, too.

REFLECTION

Notice in today's passage, the joy in heaven when someone turns from their sin to Christ is not just coming *from* the angels, but it's "*before* the angels"—in front of them. Who was it dancing most extravagantly in heaven when you first cried out for salvation? Who is it, then, that celebrates the most when you confess your sin as you seek to turn away from it? In what ways are confession and repentance positive actions worth celebrating? (Read all of Luke 15 for further reflection.)

In what ways is a testimony of a person trusting in Jesus, and the baptism that signifies this, cause for our celebration? How is our participation in the new covenant meal—the Lord's table, communion—a shared celebration rather than a time to drown in our guilt?

PART NINE

LOVE'S LIVING LETTERS

At this point in my life I know that God fills me with love,
overfills me with love, because it's supposed to spill over.
It's meant to fill the cups of others.[117]

VANEETHA RENDALL RISNER

117 Vaneetha Rendall Risner, *Walking Through Fire: A Memoir of Loss and Redemption* (Nashville, TN: Thomas Nelson, 2021), 238.

Just an Arrow

He had his eyes set
beyond shadows and leaves
trees blended together
a dark forest filled with fog
would not block his purpose
for he had determined
to never be filled with regret.

So he took his next step
stealth and precision
adrenaline pulsing through
his veins as his
passionate pursuit remained
and his aim was to shoot
his target: living flesh.

Breathing harder
he next stretched
behind his back
where his quiver was set,
filled with arrows,
he would pick purposefully with wisdom
Yes! There it was
once broken, still homely
but ready as he saw fit
in his hand safely gripped
for a plan that it
certainly could not fully know
    just an arrow
    just an arrow
just another tree in the forest once
not much different than the rest of the
    bunch . . .

But for the warrior,
suffering more than splinters to cut
it from its roots
to shave, shape, and smoothen it
until fit to be used
and quiver-bound
placed next to the rest
of his arrows where it
bounced around, bumping and being
    bumped
feeling the friction as the warrior
    would run
his course
through various Winters
while it would shiver,
astounding—it found warmth
while brushed up against
the rest of them
carried on the warrior's back
    just a pack of arrows
    just a pack of arrows
once useless but
just what he would use
to prove his wisdom
his manifold perfections
skilled at war
he was the most hated
(yet undefeated)
and his aim now was to take this
arrow and aim it, straight
into the heart of a stranger
in a land once unendangered
which the warrior had founded, but

which was occupied by brazen invaders
left without excuse
for their intrusion, and
ignorant of his pursuit

So while stripped from its
necessarily temporary abode,
the arrow knew its time had come to fly
to say goodbye to those
other arrows it had come to know
for that season.

And no one could know
exactly what that arrow felt
stripped of its prior position
and pressed against the tension
ready to release it
into the outer darkness
while it
left the fellowship within the quiver,
it's a wonder
    if arrows could cry
    if arrows could cry
how their tears must have mingled with
    joy and excitement
that their fellow arrow was flying
with the force of its master's mission,
but isn't it interesting
that arrow's perspective:
alone, cold wind piercing its sides
zooming through the forest ,
shapeless forms morphing
from one appearance to the next
meshing colors into indefinite hues

all at a dizzying speed—
but *it knew*. It knew
the warrior's view
was perfect
and his aim flawless
and soon enough
that arrow reached the outer darkness
scathed from the journey, but
sharp enough to break the skin
of the oblivious invader man
piercing into the lifeless, cold stone
in his upper left chest.

What a gruesome ministry of death
that arrow would have had
had that stone in his chest
not miraculously transformed
into living flesh—
a mysterious work,
which that arrow
    just an arrow,
could never be adequate enough
to perform.

But for the warrior, envisioning more
than vengeance against his enemies
but a life-giving ministry:

shooting his arrows
into the outer darkness
to hit
exactly who he picked

to live.

The Promised Power to Love

God's love has been poured into our hearts
through the Holy Spirit who has been given to us.

ROMANS 5:5

When Jesus had sent His disciples throughout Israel to cast out the kingdom of darkness, it was by His power (Matt. 10:5–8). But now He was back in heaven, exalted at the right hand of God the Father. How could they do this without Him here?

Jesus told them to wait for "the Helper, the Holy Spirit" (John 14:26)—Jesus' authoritative, ever-present help for His followers, even "to the end of the age" (Matt. 28:20). So, waiting in faith for this promise, about 120 of Jesus' followers committed themselves to prayer in Jerusalem (Acts 1:14). Pentecost was a Jewish harvest festival, celebrated about fifty days after the Passover. It likely coincided with the time the children of Israel received the Mosaic law at Mount Sinai, about fifty days after the exodus. Now, the greater exodus had occurred, Christ having become the sacrificial Passover Lamb who frees us from slavery to evil. And fifty days after this? The law didn't come down, but the Spirit did!

This resolved the problem Moses saw when the law had been given (Deut. 29:4), as well as the promise he communicated: "the LORD your God will circumcise your heart and the heart of your offspring, so that you will love the LORD your God with all your heart and with all your soul, that you may live" (Deut. 30:6). God had said through the prophet Ezekiel, "I will remove the heart of stone from your flesh and give you a heart of flesh. And I will put my Spirit within you, and cause you to walk in my statutes and be careful to obey my rules" (Ezek. 36:26–27). This is the promise of the new covenant: "I will put my law within them, and I will write it on their hearts" (Jer. 31:33). Pentecost was when the historic promises of God avalanched on the followers of His Son, empowering them to witness, in word and deed, to His love (Acts 2).

Christ's resurrection secured the dawning of a new day, a new kind of humanity—the "Israel of God" (Gal. 6:16)—from every nation, tongue, and tribe. So now, "if anyone is in Christ, he is a new creation. The old has passed away; behold, the new has come" (2 Cor. 5:17). Just as creation was an overflow of His Triune love, so now we—His new creation—have God's love "poured into our hearts through His Spirit," helping us to know His love for us and helping us exemplify that love as Christ did.[118] The Spirit, actively working since creation (Gen. 1:2), had now come at Pentecost in a new way, signifying "the last days" (Heb. 1:2)—the church age—in which God's people are marked by God's enduring love. We now have the privilege of creatively participating in God's new creation—coauthoring with our loving Author—until its full realization at His return. How? By the Spirit, God's power to love.

REFLECTION

The disciples understood waiting for God not as passivity but as an active devotion to daily prayer. How does an active prayer life help us experience God's love and empower us to share His love with others? See Ephesians 3:14–19; 6:10–20; Romans 8:26; Jude 1:17–21.

---

118 See my children's book, *Love Can: A Story of God's Superpower Helper* (Eugene, OR: Harvest House Publishers, 2023).

Coauthors, Wounded and Loved

Who shall separate us from the love of Christ? Shall tribulation,
or distress, or persecution, or famine, or nakedness, or danger, or sword?
As it is written, "For your sake we are being killed all the day long;
we are regarded as sheep to be slaughtered." No, in all these things
we are more than conquerors through him who loved us.

ROMANS 8:35–37

Artist and author Makoto Fujimura tells us, "In the Christian journey, the greatest triumph, the bodily resurrection of Christ from the grave, is not the 'happy ending' of a fairy tale, but only the beginning of the New with the entry point being suffering and persecution."[119] When the Spirit moves powerfully, so do the dark forces of evil (2 Tim. 3:12). This is evident in Acts, which chronicles the spread of Christ's kingdom through the persecuted church. But Christ handles our worst wounds with conquering love to make us active participants in His new creation.

God used a Pharisee named Saul (Paul), who was actively persecuting the church, to become a Christ follower and spread His love to the Gentiles (Acts 9–28). Paul, along with the rest of the apostles, suffered much persecution. Yet they knew their many afflictions were a distinguishing mark of a valid ministry (2 Cor. 6:4–10). It is the enduring joy and audacious determination to continue worshiping Jesus and caring for our enemies

---

119 Makoto Fujimura, *Art and Faith: A Theology of Making* (New Haven, CT: Yale University Press; First Edition, 2021), 41.

that separates Christian love from any other (Acts 5:40–42). This is a love of faithfulness, not dominance. This is a sacrificial love empowered by the Spirit, strengthened by our praying together, learning from God's Word together, and participating in the new covenant meal together (Acts 2:42).

This love is emboldened when we embrace the fact that Christ, in His resurrected body, still bears His wounds (John 20:7). Christ's wounds were His active participation, through suffering, in the new creation He was bringing (John 12:24). Likewise, our wounds from "all kinds of trials" (1 Peter 1:6 NIV) are the means by which God intends to keep writing His love story through us. Scripture's story doesn't romanticize pain as if it isn't painful. But it shows us Christ doesn't despise our wounds. He deals gently with them, transforming us *through* them so we can co-create with the Great Wounded Artist in His new creation—bringing new life out of the broken all around us.

Blessed are those who are willing to mourn every aspect of their brokenness. Why? That's how out-of-this-world comfort comes (Matt. 5:4). When we begin to embrace our wounds, we begin to walk in the path of Christ with the agency our Loving Author always intended for us as His coauthors in the grand drama of His love. Conquered by His love *in* our suffering, we become something "more than conquerors."

REFLECTION

Oftentimes, it's our teary eyes that help us see Christ more clearly. What are the wounds in your story you've seen God use to create something new in or through you? What are the wounds you still need Christ to touch?

Ode to Jon

This is my husband.
the one who sits with me at odd hours
under white fluorescent ER lights
rubs my back when it's debilitating all night
holds my drooping hand when the nurse declares
"pregnancy test is negative. anyway, on to x-rays."
a gentle presence in the room the last two years
of my stretch-marked body exposed, poked
and prodded by folks
who say "your insurance the same?"
prays over me while my body shakes
at potential diagnoses and my own mortality
(wondering, "will i really die today?" wondering if he
wonders the same behind that steady gaze)
shows up to the hospital next day
at 6 a.m. just to be close
(visiting hours aren't 'til 1 p.m.)
the one who uses his voice to advocate
when certain doctors who shall. not. be. named.
dismiss my questions and pain and insinuate
my inflamed lungs are from abusing drugs—
stereotype much?
(side note: please, PLEASE believe black women when we
tell you something's wrong and it's unbearable.
we—i—have no interest in playing superwoman.
we—i—just want to heal.)
the one who, too, applauds the workers who,
with tender words and touch, care for his beloved.
the one who looks me in the eye and says
"let me be your Aaron."

"i'll communicate and send updates on your behalf."
the one who sees i need to sleep on the couch tonight
propped up in order to breathe
and—without a word—plops himself on the floor
to sleep downstairs next to me.
This is my husband.
(when my body is broken, he's broken with me.)
he's asleep. and i should be.
but i keep wondering: how'd i get this lucky?

— *the real luck is love*

Shaping the New Creation with Love

Mankind, he has told each of you what is good
and what it is the LORD requires of you:
to act justly, to love faithfulness, and to walk humbly with your God.

MICAH 6:8 CSB

Christ said He would bring about His new creation like this: "unless a grain of wheat falls into the earth and dies, it remains alone; but if it dies, it bears much fruit" (John 12:24). Dying, it multiplies into new life—many new lives!—greater than its original glory.

We're not returning to Eden but moving toward the greater Eden—more glorious in every respect (Rev. 21:1–2). We're not passively waiting for Christ's return, as though our work toward justice and equity, evangelism, and day-to-day tasks are meaningless, like polishing a sinking ship. Far from it! God isn't doing away with His creation any more than He did away with Christ's crucified body—He's resurrecting it! As Christ followers we have the distinct privilege of daily engaging in creative-redemptive acts that bring renewal so that Christ's new creation beautifully breaks through the humdrum, the tragic, and the unjust realities we live in.

What's our participation in the new creation like? It's like how enslaved Africans in the mines of Colombia, bound by chains on their feet, created a dance of small foot movements called *cumbia*—a joyful dance birthed through their devalued bodies in the darkness of their oppression.[120] It's like how Japanese *kintsugi* artists take broken tea ware pieces and carefully overlay the cracks with gold, creating an even more beautiful masterpiece. It's like how enslaved Africans in the US took the unwanted scraps of their enslavers to create soul food. It's like how my Filipina tita (aunt) takes people's dying plants and, with sweat and loving attention, revives them—more lush than ever. These are not only parables of how God is working the new creation *in us*. But we ourselves are living parables of God's love story: He's shaping the new creation *through* us (1 Cor. 3:5–15)!

Imagine a world-renowned painter being so moved by her four-year-old daughter's crayon scribblings of a palm tree, that she uses her daughter's art as the inspiration behind her next masterpiece.[121] God will allow the "glory and honor" of the nations to be taken into the New Jerusalem (Rev. 21:22–26)! He doesn't dismiss your acts of *hesed* (love and justice) here and now, however insufficient they may be compared to His (1 Cor. 15:58). What is our love compared to His?! Yet He leans in with attentive love, honoring us for every bit of our faithfulness: "Well done, good and faithful servant. You have been faithful over a little; I will set you over much" (Matt. 25:21).

Being shaped by His story of love, we then coauthor with Him as we "do everything in love" (1 Cor. 16:14 CSB)—braiding hair, cooking, community-building, creating art, peacemaking, praying, and proclaiming His kingdom. And, incredibly, God is moved by our acts of love—enough to shape eternity by them.

REFLECTION

How might the Father's delight in our imperfect acts of love—like a father beaming with pride at his daughter's lopsided cartwheel—liberate us to be "zealous for good works" (Titus 2:14) without overly stressing if we're doing it perfectly?

---

120 Jon Aragon, "Double Punishment: Immigration and Anti-Blackness" (Oct. 23, 2020), WorldOutspoken.com, https://www.worldoutspoken.com/articles-blog/double-punishment-immigration-and-anti-blackness.

121 I borrow this (admittedly insufficient) analogy from a similar analogy in Makoto Fujimua's book *Art and Faith: A Theology of Making* (New Haven, CT: Yale University Press; First Edition, 2021).

One Day You're Gonna Understand
(Portrait of Jael, age 7)[122]

In high school, I wore out *The Mis-
education of Lauryn Hill*.
belted out ballads, as if
I, too, had loved and lost (I had not)
blasted her songs
from speakers to float on
stories and melodies.
I remember how she said,
"One day you're gonna understand"
before serenading her baby son, Zion.
She may as well have sung
that to me.

One day I'd understand, I'd get it:
I'll never really "get it"
never bottle the miracle of life
in your eyes
never out-imagine
your seven-year-old mind
never outrun
how fast you grow (without permission)
never know how to answer
your every question.
never manufacture, merely marvel:
    your diligence, your honesty
    your passion for Nutcracker,
        specifically Balanchine's
    the way you say, "that music does
        something in me!"
    your NYC ballet school dreams

coinciding with
your board-breaking karate kicks
proclaiming you're a "self-taught"
    pianist
soccer training with Papi
never-not knocking on neighbors'
    doors to play
singing loudly while you bathe
embracing your "curly hair magic"
much younger than when I did
your world-class bedtime stalling
    tactics.

I thought we'd have a bunch of you
little gap-toothed
3C-curly heads
tearing up the living room
but "one day you're gonna understand,"
Ms. Lauryn Hill said
and I do:
there's multitudes in you
a whole universe to explore
and
"I've never been in love like this before."

Would I serenade you with *my* script,
some karaoke for you to sing
my dreams, *my* hopes, *my* wishes?
Wouldn't the One who sang
solar systems into existence

---

122 A poem-in-conversation with Lauryn Hill's song "To Zion (feat. Carlos Santana)" from her solo
    studio album *The Miseducation of Lauryn Hill* (Ruffhouse Records and Columbia Records, 1998).

outright out-write my limited lyrics?
would I ever pretend to ghostwrite
the *poema* that's really His?
"one day you're gonna understand"
why, instead,
I weep a million "thank yous"
just to be in the room
as He composes
melody, story, song . . . in you
because "now the joy of my world" is in
knowing you beyond
the place you'll call me "Mom"
but "sister" instead.

We'll sing to the aim of all odes
in the New Jerusalem—
yes, the whole earth the Holy Land—
and "one day you're gonna understand"
I wasn't conducting a thing, little one.

just marching with you, His song,
to beautiful, beautiful Zion.

Missing the Mark of Love

If I speak in the tongues of men and of angels, but have not love,
I am a noisy gong or a clanging cymbal. And if I have prophetic powers,
and understand all mysteries and all knowledge, and if I have all faith,
so as to remove mountains, but have not love, I am nothing.
If I give away all I have, and if I deliver up my body to be burned,
but have not love, I gain nothing.

I CORINTHIANS 13:1–3

The climax of any great epic doesn't end the story; it changes the reality of everything that follows it. If the cross and resurrection of Christ is the climax of God's love story, then how we live now must be shaped by that climax. "If anyone would come after me, let him deny himself and take up his cross daily and follow me," Jesus said (Luke 9:23). But it's all too easy for us, myself very much included, to imagine faithfulness as something other than humble suffering for the good of others on the margins of the empires we live in. The church in Corinth also struggled to live every aspect of their lives shaped by the climax of God's love story.

They were divided over their allegiance to popular Bible teachers—those "super-apostles" as Paul sarcastically calls them (2 Cor. 11:5). Don't we do the same thing today with our obsession over celebrity pastors and Christian artists, assuming their influence absolves them of exploitation, abuse, or arrogance? Don't we sometimes forget that leadership, as Jesus modeled, is actually service and not celebrity? That prominence, wealth, and eloquence are *not* the markers of a powerful (or even valid) ministry (1 Cor. 1–4)?

They were using sex in ways God didn't design it because they figured, *Hey, we're free in Christ, right? Why should it matter what I do with my body?* Don't we sometimes think in the same way—watching and reading pornography, acting out on sexual desires outside of marriage? Have we forgotten that Christ's resurrection means He cares very much about the human body and sexual integrity? That He died for our sexual brokenness, and now our bodies are the temple of His holy presence (1 Cor. 5–7)?

They were arguing about eating meat that had been sacrificed to false gods. Even though these false gods were, well, false, what mattered was whether eating or abstaining from that meat would help others know the truth about Jesus. Don't we sometimes forget that love requires us to sacrifice our preferences for the sake of others' needs—as Jesus did for us (1 Cor. 8–10)?

And then there was the gathering of the believers, filled with chaos as people interrupted each other to speak in different languages and teach; and filled with classism as the wealthy used the new covenant meal in a way that disregarded the needs of the poor (1 Cor. 11–14). It's in the midst of all this confusion that Paul proclaims that famous love poem: "Love is patient, love is kind," and so on in 1 Corinthians 13. He was trying to help them see that this love story of Christ is a multifaceted story, sufficient to address their complex, multifaceted lives. This good news of Jesus is anchored in His self-giving love, so that we could embody that same love.

Sacrificial, humble love for the building up of others is the key marker of the new creation bursting into our world, both in and through us.

REFLECTION

I admit I tremble as I write this particular meditation. I know I haven't lived up to the love story of Christ in so many ways that 1 Corinthians espouses. Perhaps you feel the same way. Maybe a part of your story growing up included being corrected with harshness or even emotional abuse. That likely affects how you receive the Spirit's conviction now. How might it be helpful for us to feel the Spirit's conviction as God's invitation *into* a greater experience of His love, rather than a judge's hammer of condemnation? See Luke 18:9–14; 1 John 1:9.

He Loves Me,
He Loves Me Not?

So we have come to know and to believe the love that God has for us.
God is love, and whoever abides in love abides in God, and God abides in him.
By this is love perfected with us, so that we may have confidence
for the day of judgment, because as he is so also are we in this world.
There is no fear in love, but perfect love casts out fear.
For fear has to do with punishment, and whoever fears
has not been perfected in love. We love because he first loved us.

I JOHN 4:16-19

The apostles were now older. With their deaths (many of them martyred), this world would lose its eyewitnesses to Jesus' life, death, and resurrection. The church would soon be led by the next generation of disciples.

But there were teachers in the early church who had turned away from belief in the Jesus the apostles knew and preached, actively making disciples of a whole different Jesus. The believers needed to be assured that the Jesus they were living for, suffering persecution for, and hoping in was the true Jesus. Have you ever wondered the same? Between every social media "expert," every brand of Christianity, every new bestseller with the secret to "true" spirituality, and our own internal wavering, each day can feel like that flower game—picking off each petal with, "He loves me. He loves me not. . ." John didn't want us to have to live like this. His words offer certainty of our faith and God's love for us.

But what about all these different Jesuses I hear about? Listen to the teachers who tell the story of Jesus as the promised Messiah (Christ), the Son of God—the One who came into our world, fully God and fully man (1 John 2:22; 4:2, 15). Listen to the ones who do not stray from the apostles' teachings as written in the New Testament about who Jesus is (1 John 4:1–6). If those teachers make it seem like they never sin (1 John 1:8–10), or if they live in constant sin they justify instead of repenting from (1 John 2:3–6), they do not know the true Jesus. If they're more marked by the need to be right and the need to have a position of prominence and leadership (dominance) rather than a sacrificial, others-focused love (faithfulness), they do not know the One who gave His life for us in love (1 John 3:10–18).

What about if I sin again and again? Remember that God, who is light (1 John 1:5), does care about our moral integrity; but a huge part of that moral integrity is an active practice of confessing your sin to God, who is "faithful and just to forgive us our sins and to cleanse us from all unrighteousness" (1 John 1:9; 2:1–2). You can "walk in the light" (1 John 1:7) by active obedience to God's Word, sacrificially loving others, and confessing your sin when you fail.

What if, despite all this, my own heart condemns me, and I can't shake the feeling I'm doomed? Three witnesses reassure us: belief in the apostles' teaching, going back to the Scripture's story of Jesus; the Holy Spirit's presence within us (1 John 4:13); and a life of increasing love for God expressed in our love for others (1 John 3:23). These things give our hearts reassurance in God's love, no matter what accusations we receive. And "whenever our heart condemns us, God is greater than our heart, and he knows everything" (1 John 3:20).

Our hearts can be fickle things (ask me how I know). Our stories are complex, layered with our own corruption, the evil done to us, and confusion in the world around us. But there is no one more committed to your sanctification—your being made to look more and more like Christ in the way you love—than God Himself. When your heavenly Father looks at you, He beholds the perfection of His Beloved Son. He will stop loving you as soon as He stops loving His Son. When you fail, as every disciple does, run back to God as your loving Father who will not deny Himself—His very Spirit in you.

May His perfect love for you continue to cast out all fear of condemnation, 'til you can confidently say, "He loves me. He loves me. He loves me."

REFLECTION

What are the things that tend to make you feel uneasy or unassured about God's love?

A Loving Author,
His Living Letters

For I am sure that neither death nor life, nor angels nor rulers,
nor things present nor things to come, nor powers, nor height nor depth,
nor anything else in all creation, will be able to separate us
from the love of God in Christ Jesus our Lord.

ROMANS 8:38–39

There are times I wish God would have just beamed me up as soon as I had first trusted in His Son. There are times life has felt meaningless, or like I'm one big cosmic joke. But one of the most incredible things about our Loving Author is that He brings us into His great love story, not only as His subjects but as His coauthors. He shows us how much our lives matter to Him. In Christ, God makes us a new kind of humanity—living letters of His love (2 Cor. 3:3).

Eager to bless, He didn't spare any expense—even His priceless Son—to bring you into His family. As His adopted child (like a firstborn son in ancient times), you, like Christ, are an heir of God, eternally known and loved (Rom. 8:16–17). You can be confident when you pray because He already spent heaven's greatest treasure on you (Rom. 8:32). Love is lavish like that; it doesn't hold back.

Eager to partner with you in shaping His new creation, He honors even your seemingly small acts of love (Matt. 25:31–40). As you let Christ touch your wounds with His scarred hands, He brings new life out of your million little deaths on the path to the true Promised Land (Heb. 12:22). Love is attentive like that. It leans in, dignifying every aspect of our existence.

Eager to keep His promises, He uses every sunny and dark night of the soul as chapters in the grand epic of your life story—all working "together for good" (Rom. 8:28). All of it accomplishing His loving purpose to see you "glorified" in the fullness of your humanity, bearing the Christlikeness He planned for you since before creation (Rom. 8:29–30). Love is faithful like that. It writes redemptively, refusing to waste any tear along the way.

Eager to bring more people into His love, He has made you into His holy temple, housing His very Spirit (1 Cor. 6:19; cf. 1 Peter 2:5), so that how you "pick up the pen" and write—how you live here and now—can be done in holy love. Scripture's story about Jesus wasn't meant to be read like your favorite fiction novel. It is meant to *read you*—exposing God's heart and yours, transforming yours to be more like His (Heb. 4:12). Love is infectious like that. It replicates and spreads.

But perhaps the greatest news is that God's love story doesn't end with your legacy. Love isn't bound by time. In fact, love redeems time—making it work backwards, as it were, transforming every wound into an incomparable glory in eternity (Rom. 8:18; 2 Cor. 4:17). Love is timeless like that. It is stronger than death.

And if that's the case, then this isn't the end of the story, is it?

PART TEN

THE COMMUNITY OF LOVE
AND YOUR STORY'S
NON-ENDING END

The crown of eternal life for those who love Him,
and also for those who come to love Him,
through our surrender to a whole-life witness.[123]

K. A. ELLIS

123 K. A. Ellis, *Wisdom's Call: 100 Meditations for a Life in Christ* (Chicago, IL: Moody Publishers, 2023), 181.

Love Flips the Script

*"Worthy is the Lamb who was slain, to receive power and wealth
and wisdom and might and honor and glory and blessing!"*

REVELATION 5:12

Seven churches in Asia, under Roman colonization and persecution,
were the first to receive a prophetic letter from the apostle John—"the
revelation of Jesus Christ" (Rev. 1:1). Some had become indifferent because
of their riches. Others were morally compromised. Others were faithful
under persecution. Jesus needed them to know things were going to get
even more difficult, but that the worst wouldn't be the end of the story
(Rev. 1–3). We, too, need the blessing this prophecy offers to all who read it
and live it out (Rev. 1:3). We need its symbolic vision of "him who loves us
and has freed us from our sins by his blood" (Rev. 1:5) so we can overcome
every bit of lovelessness, both within and without.

It helps to remember that Revelation is written in the Jewish literary
style (genre) of apocalypse. Author and Bible teacher Kristie Anyabwile
reminds us, "Imagery and symbolism are the two main literary features of
apocalyptic literature."[124] Remember how so many subplots and prophetic
images were left unresolved at the end of the Old Testament? The book
of Revelation is a masterpiece of symbolism with its characters and numbers harking back to a ton of these Old Testament prophecies (like Daniel,

---

124 Kristie Anyabwile, *Literarily: How Understanding Bible Genres Transforms Bible Study* (Chicago, IL:
Moody Publishers, 2022), 134.

Ezekiel, and Zechariah), showing how God will fulfill every promise He ever made. But *how* He does it is what's most astonishing.

Through multiple visions about divine judgment over evil, the book keeps returning to its main symbol. John hears of the conquering King, "the Lion of the tribe of Judah" (Rev. 5:5; cf. Gen. 49:9). But what he sees is "a Lamb standing, as though it had been slain" (Rev. 5:6). That slain (slaughtered) lamb leads a multiethnic army (Rev. 7; cf. Gen. 17:4). The great plot twist of history is that evil was conquered—not by military might, conquest, colonization, or culture wars, but by the self-giving love of our Passover Lamb, the Lord Jesus Christ. For this very reason He is showered in heaven's praise!

But we're not mere spectators in God's great epic. The script was set when humanity first rebelled in Eden, trading self-achieved power for freely given love. The offspring of the serpent would wage war with the offspring of Eve (Rev. 12:3; Gen. 3:15). But those who overcome are not the ones who wage war as the world does—with prominence, opulence, and dominance. The conquerors are the ones who "follow the Lamb wherever he goes" (Rev. 14:4)—through enemy-loving suffering, *and then* into vindicating glory (Rev. 12:11; cf. Rom. 16:20). History's script is simply this: empires will continue to empire, corrupting love and tempting us to do the same. But God's love flips the script—first through the Lamb, then also through us!

Like the Lamb, our apparent weakness will be our glory. Our wounds, like His, will be honored. Our laments will turn into everlasting praise. Our stories will be expressions of God's love, especially for our enemies—even unto death. Why? Because death is just the first step toward a glorious resurrection.

As it turns out, Love held the script rights the whole time.

REFLECTION

How is God's love through Scripture's story flipping the script in how you approach suffering, leadership, failure, and success?

The Great Wedding Feast, The Forever Marriage

*"Let us rejoice and exult
and give him the glory,
for the marriage of the Lamb has come,
and his Bride has made herself ready"*

REVELATION 19:7

We can't possibly talk about God's love without a good glimpse at the great marriage feast of the Lamb (Christ) and His Bride (the church). The apostle John heard "what seemed to be the voice of a great multitude," proclaiming praise to God "for the marriage of the Lamb has come, and his Bride has made herself ready" (Rev. 19:6–7). An angel then told him, "'Write this: Blessed are those who are invited to the marriage supper of the Lamb'" (Rev. 19:9).

Jesus said that "in the resurrection they neither marry nor are given in marriage" (Matt. 22:30). But He also said the kingdom could be compared to being invited by a king to the wedding feast of his son (Matt. 22:1–14; cf. Matt. 25:1–13). So in one sense, singleness is our destiny; but in another sense, "your Maker is your husband" (Isa. 54:5). Despite being like the prophet Hosea's unfaithful bride, we were "granted" (given as a gift) the opportunity through Christ to clothe our naked shame with "fine linen," which is "the righteous deeds of the saints," so we can fulfill

Isaiah's prophecy: "he has covered me with the robe of righteousness" (Isa. 61:10). The apostle Paul, referencing the first marriage between Adam and Eve (Gen. 2:18–25), said marriage itself is actually a mystery—a truth once hidden, now revealed in Christ—about the nature of union—two becoming one—of Christ and His church (Eph. 5:22–33). Like a newlywed we'll sing, "I am my beloved's, and his desire is for me" (Song 7:10 NASB).

The consummation of God's love story is a wedding feast! But the end of history is actually a new beginning—a forever marriage of heaven and earth.

> Then I saw a new heaven and a new earth, for the first heaven and the first earth had passed away, and the sea was no more. And I saw the holy city, new Jerusalem, coming down out of heaven from God, prepared as a bride adorned for her husband. And I heard a loud voice from the throne saying, "Behold, the dwelling place of God is with man. He will dwell with them, and they will be his people, and God himself will be with them as their God. He will wipe away every tear from their eyes, and death shall be no more, neither shall there be mourning, nor crying, nor pain anymore, for the former things have passed away."
> (Rev. 21:1–4)

This unearthing of God's love story brings together Scripture's themes beautifully. When Christ returns and resurrects us into our glorified bodies, we will see that the new creation *is* the new heaven and the new earth (Isa. 65:17; Rev. 21:1), *which is actually* the new garden of Eden (Gen. 2; Ezek. 47; Rev. 22:1–3), *which is actually* the New Jerusalem (Isa. 2; Zeph. 3; Heb. 12:22; Rev. 21:2), *which is actually* the whole cosmos! The city of God (Zion) will be the whole earth, and that city won't need a temple "for its temple is the Lord God the Almighty and the Lamb" (Rev. 21:22). What Jesus told us to pray—"Your kingdom come, your will be done, on earth as it is in heaven" (Matt. 6:10)—will come true. How? All the earth will become heaven!

What a great marriage feast! What a glorious Bridegroom! Ah, but the wedding is just the beginning of a marriage—isn't it?

The Hands of Time

I long for the day
when I can say to your face
"I love you"
and know that in covenant we stand
even as we walk
    my hand in your hand
    knowing time is all but sure,
but seeking to serve the One who
    holds time in His hands,
and taking the
    time He gives us
to love—
not just with the words of our tongues,
  but
building His kingdom
    with our hands
like the woman in Proverbs 31.
Me to submit to you,
and you to love me
as Christ loved the church.
I wait patiently in faith
in the God who loved me first . . .
    Even before time
He chose me to be
blameless and holy,
in love He chose me.
    And in the fullness of time
He did more than just
    reach out His hand,
but
let my sin slam nails
    through His Son's hands
to demonstrate His love

and complete His eternal plan.
Then, allow me to breathe
2,000 years later,
    let me reach my hands
toward all kinds of sin
(since birth my natural inclination
was to evade Him)
Then He sent His Spirit
    right on time
to awaken me from my sleep,
raise me from the dead,
allow my eyes to see,
all that Jesus did . . . was for *me*.

His Word gave life to me! It's like He
held my heart of stone
    in His hand
and it became flesh
and began to beat to a chant,
saying,
"Worthy is the Lamb, slain for my sins!"

And I don't totally understand
and could never fully explain His love
    even if I had time,
But His plan and His promise is that
    time (as we know it)
    will end . . .

And then the marriage feast
of the Lamb and His Bride will
    commence.
    He'll take His Bride's hand
and she'll remember His sacrifice

His blood shed to purchase her
Oh, the words that He spoke to her
that cleansed her within!
The Church is Christ's Bride
and she'll be dressed in righteousness,
    clean and bright.
They'll say, "Yes! She's made herself
    ready!"
But it will be He who presents her to
    Himself spotless
because He said He
loves us to the end
is more than a best friend
the Lover of our souls
wrote us a love letter
    with His hand
pursues our hearts
and then loves to be pursued
This is a Divine Romance.

So, *mi amor*, I love you so much
but our love and union
is a temporary covenant
made to represent
    a timeless union
    no human hand can ruin.
I will fail you much more than once,
and your love toward me won't be
    perfect, but
we'll be united as one
to be further purged of our impurities
and prepared for *our* perfect Bridegroom.

So let's be like
    the hands on a clock
when our flesh becomes one
    as if time could stop
when midnight comes.
Because at midnight the clock chimes
with a beautiful sound that fills the
    house,
        and the hands of time
        are united for a moment
only able to point upward
to the God who sits forever enthroned in
the glory of His splendor.

Our marriage is only for a moment.
May our union 'til death
point the world to Jesus Christ
that He may be glorified.
Our lives are not our own
through creation and atonement.

We exist to live and to know
His Divine Romance.

Love Never Ends,
Neither Does Your Story

The Spirit and the Bride say, "Come."
And let the one who hears say, "Come."
And let the one who is thirsty come;
let the one who desires take the water of life without price.

REVELATION 22:17

Earlier in this book, I said that Scripture's story is not only the great-est love story ever told—it's also the longest. That's not only because the Bible contains the collected writings of about forty different authors who wrote on three different continents over a span of about 1,500 years. Scripture's story is actually the longest story ever told because where it should say "The End," there's really a "To Be Continued . . ."—through you!

Scripture's story began with "God's people living in God's place with full access to his presence."[125] Then from creation came corruption. But God had always planned a great redemption and new creation. From one man (Noah) came a family (Abraham), from which came a nation (Israel), through which all nations (the church) are blessed. So . . . the end? Not exactly. The end of Scripture's story is an invitation to "Come!"

With your self-made entitlement? With your self-manufactured righ-teousness because you're not as bad as someone else? With your ministry

---

125 Sandra L. Richter, *The Epic of Eden: A Christian Entry into the Old Testament* (Downers Grove, IL: IVP Academic, 2008), 118.

credentials and church activity? No, no, no! You bring water only one gift: your thirst. What gives us the right to "see his face" and yet live? (See Rev. 22:4; cf. Ex. 33:20.) Faith in the one who "is love" (1 John 4:8) and who showed His love for us by laying His life down to make us His friends. So bring nothing but your thirst—your need, your inability, your desperation. In exchange, He gives "the water of life without price."

Come! Drink from the waters of God's love since before time and throughout history.

Come! Refresh yourself in the water of life—free for us, purchased by His blood.

> Come!
> Find yourself so deeply loved,
> you can't help but
> join the chorus of
> "Come!"

The perfect unity of Heaven and earth will unfold timelessly as we use every God-given gift, talent, and treasure to explore and expand His endless glory as we (yes, *we*) lovingly "reign forever and ever" (Rev. 22:5) with "Jesus Christ the faithful witness, the firstborn of the dead, and the ruler of kings on earth" (Rev. 1:5). So we pray, "Amen. Come, Lord Jesus!" (Rev. 22:20).

And so, the end of God's great love epic in Scripture is not *really* the end, is it? "Love never ends" (1 Cor. 13:8). And so, neither does this love story. And so, beloved, neither does yours.

REFLECTION

What hope might well up in your heart as you reflect on the endless nature of your love story with God?

If I Were a Tree

Agh! What of this mess?
Strange sap melting back
into stinging cracks
torn upon my trunk upholding
choking, frozen easily broken branch
lightning strikes and hollow blows
from feigned friends
only expose my own deep-rooted
deficiencies within,
just fertile soil for further sin.

But what of this Gardener God-man?
He knows trees, He foreknew me
And now I know him.
He's at work,
uprooting, consuming
that bitterness rooted beneath
my callus bark ridge.
And I recall, given gall
He gave me figs.
My risen Judge, His
tree-nailed wrists
bearing marks of His passion—
those scars? My sin against Him
are ornaments of grace,
worn and adored in Heaven.

His wounds, His weapons
defeating death's herbicide-like sting.
So I, this mess, will sing
of His thorn-crowned compassion.

Cursed for the Fall on a tree
to resurrect and
awaken us Spring:
beautifully fruitful, His vineyard green.

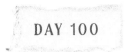

A Loving Author,
Unique Stories Unified by Love

Oh give thanks to the LORD, *for he is good,*
for his steadfast love endures forever!
Let the redeemed of the LORD *say so,*
whom he has redeemed from trouble
and gathered in from the lands,
from the east and from the west,
from the north and from the south.

PSALM 107:1–3

My husband, Jon, often describes God's diverse, global family (the church) as a gorgeous garden. Some plants bear fruit, some vegetables, others bloom flowers—each with its own scent. Likewise, we each have unique stories of how God's love met us. When the Spirit of God, like wind, blows on His garden, together we spread "the fragrance of the knowledge of him everywhere" (2 Cor. 2:14). I love this illustration. I believe this is the call of Psalm 107.

Wherever you're from, go ahead and tell how God's enduring love (*hesed*) invaded your life. Pick up the pen, sharing how the Loving Author of history wrote redemption into your story. Notice how diverse this psalm's testimonies are. Some were refugees—unable to find a home, no matter where they looked (vv. 4–9). Some were imprisoned—enslaved and destined for doom (vv. 10–16). Some were at death's door—afflicted by their own bad decisions (vv. 17–22). Some were pummeled by natural disasters—losing their minds in the chaos (vv. 23–32). The greater the diversity of their stories, the more glorious their unity on this one crucial commonality: "Let them thank the LORD for his steadfast love" (vv. 8, 15, 21, 31).

So go ahead, "proclaim the excellencies of him who called you out of darkness into his marvelous light" (1 Peter 2:9). You don't need to hide from the darker parts of your story, nor your heritage or heart language. Maybe they won't make a film adaptation of your life story. So what? No testimony of God's indescribable love is boring or unworthy of its retelling. In fact, it's the uniqueness of your story that brings glory to God's multifaceted love.

The new creation is a multiethnic, multicultural family—each person maintaining their uniquely layered identities and stories, yet perfectly unified in their loving adoration of Christ (Rev. 7:9–10). The chorus of the church's song is not one of uniformity, as though Christ only died for one culture or one type of life story. Our chorus is one of perfect unity and harmony, reflecting the diverse yet unified, Triune community of love that has enveloped us into forever-love:

We are the redeemed, each a unique story
We are many, yet we are one
Each and all, conquered by Christ's love!

The psalm ends how I hope to end this book: "Whoever is wise, let him attend to these things; let them consider the steadfast love of the LORD" (Ps. 107:43)—in Scripture's story, which *is* yours.

Acknowledgments

To every person who has helped me know God's love, in word and deed: thank you.

To my family who has rallied around me, thank you. You have no idea how much healing your support and encouragement have brought me.

Jael, my beloved daughter, I don't think you'll ever fully know how much your joy, curiosity, and kindness has inspired me to "become like children" to "enter the kingdom of heaven" (Matt. 18:3).

Dad, I'm so thrilled to be growing closer and closer to you in the last few years. Thank you for your humility, gentleness, and steadfast support. May our relationship, like the mini garden you helped me start on my balcony, continue to bloom with beauty. I love you so much!

A mis queridos suegros, Pastor Isaac Aragón y Esther Aragón Isajar, que han estado presentes en mis más difíciles momentos con el mismo amor incondicional. Orando, animándome, y cocinándome el más sabroso sancocho del mundo. ¡Mil gracias!

Mom and Mo, I cannot form a sentence for you without weeping. God has done so much in our story. Thank you for being a constant encouragement to me. You're both always eager to pray, laugh, and weep along with me in every high and low.

Mom, thank you for instilling in me a love for stories and storytelling— from your dramatic (and hilariously loud) retelling of family stories, to taking me to Saturday morning story time at Barnes & Noble when I was a kid (with the very necessary purchase of hot chocolate and a croissant, of course!). You were my first editor for every school essay I wrote (I still remember your red pen), and you introduced me to the wonderful world of literature. More than that, you've exemplified the unbelievably patient love of God through all my growing pains.

Monique, we are sisters in every sense of the word. Your genuine faith in Christ is the biggest answer to prayer I've ever experienced and continue to experience. Thank you for allowing me access into your life, which has taught me so much about the tender care and love of God.

In my moments of discouragement, I've turned countless times to my husband, Jon, who has listened thoughtfully, entered courageously into my heart's darker rooms, and reminded me of the Spirit's work in my life. On many occasions of my expressing doubt and self-disdain, Jon has (after sympathizing and encouraging me) ended his exhortation with, "Oh, and don't talk about my wife like that." His loving labor in our marriage—his prayers, his emotional presence—is one of the greatest reasons I've continued writing. I love you, mi amor. Para siempre.

I've also returned to the words of my dear friend, Rafael "Rafy" Amador, who asked me throughout the last few years, "What would it look like for Quina to write—not out of fear of imperfectly proclaiming God's Word, or under the gaze of critics, but out of her safe space within God's presence?" A million thanks to my faithful friend.

I've returned to trauma therapy sessions with one of the most compassionate, intelligent women I've ever met. She embodies Proverbs 20:5 as she helps me piece parts of my stories together, discover constructive ways of caring for my nervous system, and even resolve some traumas I never imagined God would tend to. My heart bursts with gratitude for you.

I've found a wonderful Jesus community in Orlando called New Creation Fellowship. You all have no idea how much of an answered prayer you are! Thank you for your faithfulness.

Thank you to Trillia Newbell. You've exemplified so much patience and grace throughout this process. Thank you to my agent Bill Jensen and his sweet wife, Sheila. You have shared your own wounds with me, and you've spurred me on to tell the story of God's love in my life. Thank you to my editor, Pam, who worked so hard on this book for the benefit of every reader.

Thank you to my friends Taylor Turkington, Gina and Frankie Concepcion, Aja Dixon, Chelsey and Isaac Molina, Sonia Quirindongo, Nicole and Marc Diaz, Rachel Li and Steven Guo, Ike and Arianysis Todd, Rechab and Brittany Gray, and Demetrius Hicks. Your care has meant the world to me.

Inevitably, I've missed many names. Truly, words fail to convey all my thanks.

To every reader, thank you for taking the time to engage with these insufficient yet genuine meditations. I hope you've discovered the wonderful paradox Paul expresses in Ephesians 3. Even as Paul longs for the Ephesians to comprehend God's love, he tells them the love of God "surpasses knowledge." The more of His love we excavate, the more we joyfully realize we've barely scratched the surface. In other words, we can know we don't know the half of God's love, but even that ignorance—of which we're aware—leads us to erupt with joy. Whoa. Should we ever fully know all there is to know about God's love? Could the finite ever finish plumbing the depths of the infinite? Would we ever want to?

· · ·

Jesus, thank You for doing everything it took to bring me by Your side forever. I offer this book as an imperfect labor of love with faith that You will somehow use it to conquer more curious and aching hearts, like mine, with Your unfailing love.

You finished reading!

Did this book help you in some way? If so, please consider writing an honest review wherever you purchase your books. Your review gets this book into the hands of more readers and helps us continue to create biblically faithful resources.

Moody Publishers books help fund the training of students for ministry around the world.

The **Moody Bible Institute** is one of the most well-known Christian institutions in the world, training thousands of young people to faithfully serve Christ wherever He calls them. And when you buy and read a book from Moody Publishers, you're helping make that vital ministry training possible.

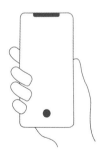

Continue to dive into the Word, *anytime, anywhere.*

Find what you need to take your next step in your walk with Christ: from uplifting music to sound preaching, our programs are designed to help you right when you need it.

Download the **Moody Radio App** and start listening today!

 MOODY Publishers

 MOODY Bible Institute

 MOODY Radio